MW00357079

FIXED INCOME INVESTMENTS

INVESTMENTS

A Personal Seminar

FIXED INCOME INVESTMENTS

A Personal Seminar

NEW YORK INSTITUTE OF FINANCE

Library of Congress Cataloging-in-Publication Data

Fixed income investments: a personal seminar.
   Includes index.
     ISBN 0-13-322207-1: $21.95
      1. Investments. 2. Finance, Personal.   I. New York Institute of Finance.
HG4521.F6142 1989
332.6'78—dc20   89-3445
                                                     CIP

© 1989 by NYIF Corp.
A Division of Simon & Schuster, Inc.
70 Pine Street, New York, NY 10270-0003

All rights reserved.
No part of this book may be reproduced
in any part or by any means
without permission in writing from the author.

This publication is designed to provide accurate and authoritative
information in regard to the subject matter covered. It is sold with the
understanding that the publisher is not engaged in rendering legal,
accounting, or other professional service. If legal service or other
expert assistance is required, the services of a competent
professional person should be sought.

—From a Declaration of Principles jointly adopted by a
Committee of the American Bar Association and a Committee
of Publishers and Associations

Printed in the United States of America

10 9 8 7 6 5 4 3 2 1

New York Institute of Finance
(NYIF Corp.)
70 Pine St.
New York, New York 10270-0003

Contents

---

3   What Is Yield?   **45**

6 U.S. Government Securities   115

7 Money Market Instruments   143

Introduction

To many people, the word "investments" is synonymous with "stock market." Yet if you totaled the trading volumes on all the stock exchanges and all other types of stock markets around the world, the sum would be dwarfed by the size and scope of the collective marketplace for fixed income investments. Every year, hundreds of billions of dollars worth of such instruments are issued by:

*U.S. corporations, which offer corporate bonds, notes, commercial paper, bankers' acceptances, and other forms of debt.

*State and local governments, which issue "municipal" bonds and several types of notes.

*The United States Treasury and other federal agencies, which are the sources of T bonds, T bills, T notes, mortgage-backed securities, and other forms of government debt.

*Overseas companies and governments, as well as international agencies such as the World Bank or European Investment Bank, whose issuances constitute the so-called Eurobond market.

In brief, fixed income investment issuance and trading constitute over 90% of all securities trading volume—worldwide.

This *Personal Seminar* enables you to participate in this huge, diverse, and rewarding market:

*Chapter 1 explains what fixed income instruments are, how they work, and what characteristics they have in common.

*Chapter 2 briefly explains each type of fixed income investment.

Chapter 3 talks about yield—what it is, how it is calculated, and what it means in terms of return.

Chapters 4, 5, and 6 go into detail about corporate bonds, municipal securities, and U.S. government instruments—how they are priced, quoted, and traded.

*Chapter 7 describes the money market and its short-term instruments.

*Chapter 8 tells you what to expect to pay or receive in accrued interest when you buy or sell fixed income instruments.

*A glossary at the end of the book provides you with quick definitions of any terms you do not understand.

Fixed Income Investments: A Personal Seminar is a cost-effective way to become conversant with the whole array of fixed income securities, one of which may well be appropriate and profitable for you.

1
Getting to Know Fixed Income Investments

The Two Major Fixed Income Markets

The global arena in which debt investments play such an important role is divided into two markets: the capital market (which also includes equity instruments) and the money market.

In the **capital market** are traded long-term debt instruments, that is, bonds, along with stocks, both common and preferred. These are vehicles by which capital is raised, though we should note at the outset that common stock is not considered a fixed income investment. The bonds traded in this market may be issued by

The U.S. Treasury, through auctions at the 12 Federal Reserve District Banks. The auctions are dominated by a group of "primary dealers" ("primary" applies to the 46 dealers that report directly and daily to the Federal Reserve System).

Federal agencies such as the Government National Mortgage Association (GNMA) and others, for example,

State and local governments—municipal issuers.

Domestic and foreign corporations.

Foreign governments.

The **money market** consists of short-term fixed income vehicles, that is, those with less than one year to maturity. This market includes bonds whose maturity is less than one year away as well as these other vehicles:

Treasury bills.

U.S. government agency notes.

Municipal notes.

Bank certificates of deposit (CDs).

Commercial paper.

Repurchase agreements (repos).

Banker's acceptances (BAs).

The money market has no specific location. Rather, it is a collection of markets comprised of

Banks in the large money centers—New York, London, Tokyo, and so on.

Over 40 government securities dealers, known as "primary dealers."

Secondary government securities dealers, those who voluntarily report their activity to the Fed and all other dealers.

Roughly a dozen commercial paper dealers.

A few banker's acceptance dealers.

A number of money brokers specializing in finding short-term funds from money market lenders and placing the funds with money market borrowers.

The most important money market brokers are based in New York and deal in **federal funds,** which represent "surplus reserves" or money that banks do not need to meet the Fed's reserve requirements. These funds are available for unsecured short-term (usually overnight) loans, usually only to banks.

Money market participants are any political or corporate entities that need to ensure having enough cash on hand to meet their expenses and to operate normally—independently of their cash flow. Participants who at any time need cash may borrow from those who have too much cash for their current needs. Thus the money market provides a pool of cash that, through its trading mechanisms, flows to those participants in need of it. For example, the money market, through repos, enable government dealers to finance their inventories of fixed income securities. The market is particularly valuable in that the instruments are perceived to entail very little risk of default, and most transactions are collateralized.

At one time money market investments were available to only the largest financial and commercial institutions. The high interest rates of the early 1980s, however, were too good to ignore. So now, through money market (mutual) funds, individual investors may enjoy the benefits of the money market: short maturities, high liquidity, and relatively low risk.

Differences from Other Markets

Stock and Bonds

So, what exactly is the difference between the stock and bond markets? The purchase of common or preferred stock represents an equity investment in the particular publicly traded company. As a stockholder, you are an owner of the company; how you fare as an investor depends on the company's success or failure. When you purchase a bond of the same publicly traded company, you acquire a debt instrument and you become a creditor of that company. The only claim you have against the company is for the face amount of the bond itself plus the interest the company has promised to pay for the use of your money, except for hybrid securities, such as convertible bonds or preferred stock.

In general, if you buy a bond, a debt is owed you by the bond's issuer. As a bond owner, you are promised a fixed payment in the form of interest, usually paid on a semiannual basis over the life of the bond. The price of the bond varies, depending on whether interest rates rise or fall. For example, if interest rates rise after you purchase a particular bond, the price of the bond you bought must fall to bring the yield (the interest payment divided by the price) into line with the prevailing yield of similar bonds. The price of a bond maturity in 30 years reacts to changes in prevailing interest rates to a greater degree than does the price of a bond coming due in a year or two. This disparity is due to the fact that the owner of a 30-year bond is exposed to the impact of the higher interest rates for a much longer time.

For the most part, bonds are liquid investment vehicles because an active marketplace exists for such investments. The liquidity varies by issuer, creditworthiness, and maturity, to name a few variables.

TRY THIS: *

Bonds differ from stocks in that
a. Bonds are sold privately between individuals, while stocks are exchange-traded.
b. Bonds can't be resold, whereas stocks can.
c. Bonds represent debt, while stocks represent ownership.
d. Bonds do not differ greatly from stocks.

HERE'S WHY:

The correct answer is (c). When you buy bonds you are actually lending money to the issuer of the bond. The debt consists of a loan from investors to bond issuers, who can be business corporations, the U.S. government, or municipalities.

Why would a publicly traded company issue bonds instead of stock? Good question. A company that goes public raises capital by

*You will be asked periodically to respond to multiple choice and other types of questions.

offering its stock through an underwriter to the investing public. When additional capital is needed, management considers a number of factors in choosing a method for raising those funds. The condition of the company, the condition of the marketplace, the nature of the project for which the funds are needed, and the internal characteristics of the particular company are some of the factors that play a role in management's decision to offer stocks or bonds.

As a company grows in size and earning power, its bonds typically become more marketable because the principal players in the bond market are large institutional investors or wealthy individuals whose major concern is to preserve their capital and to provide a predictable and adequate return for their assets. Such investors focus their attention on the company's assets and earning power rather than on future prospects. They rely on rating services such as Moody's Investor Service, Inc., and Standard & Poor's Corporation in deciding whether to purchase a particular bond or not. Thus, many newer, smaller companies are excluded completely from the bond market (except for the "junk" bond market).

Market conditions also play an important role in determining whether a company will raise capital through a bond or a stock offering. If the stock market is rising and the particular company's stock is performing well, the company's underwriter will most likely suggest a stock offering. Obviously, if the price of the company's stock is higher than normal, relatively fewer shares will have to be sold to raise the needed dollar amount, and the company's equity will be diluted to a lesser degree. In a declining market, a stock offering may be extremely difficult, if not impossible, and a bond offering may be the only route available. Also, a stock offering in a declining stock market would result in a greater dilution in the company's equity base. The current level of interest rates also plays a significant role in determining whether a stock offering or bond issue should be undertaken. If interest rates are rising or unusually high, the rate on a new bond issue (which represents interest expense to the issuing corporation) will be elevated. In such cases, a stock issue might be preferable.

The nature of the project also has a bearing on the way it will be financed. If the money to be raised is designated for a specific project, such as new plant construction or an existing plant's modernization, management and its investment banker will most likely select a bond issue because costs and returns can be specifically projected. However, if the funds are for general corporate purposes, rather than for a specific project, and if the stock market is particularly strong, an equity offering may be more appropriate.

The peculiar characteristics of the company also influence the selection of financing alternatives. Management policy may dictate that the company carry very little debt and that the bulk of funds for financing growth and expansion come from internally generated funds and equity offerings. Bank covenants may also limit additional debt. On the other hand, some corporate managements believe in the extensive use of debt and are willing to leverage (that is, borrow heavily against) corporate assets. The use of leverage has a dramatic effect because it magnifies corporate results, whether positive (increase in earnings) or negative (decline in earnings).

As an investor, you should be familiar with some terms and concepts used by management and investors when describing debt and equity financing. The **debt-to-equity ratio** comes into play whenever a decision between debt and equity financing must be made. This ratio expresses in numerical terms what percentage of a company's capital structure is represented by debt and what percentage is represented by equity. Managements seek to maintain a balance between the debt and equity components of their capital structure. For the investor, the debt-to-equity ratio gives a clue as to whether the company is excessively leveraged or is diluting its equity base by issuing too many shares. **Trading on the equity** means that a company is earning a higher rate of return in the business (equity side) than it is paying for the cost of the money it borrows (debt side). Expressed another way, trading on the equity means that the rate of return a company can earn in its business exceeds the rate of interest it has to pay to borrow the funds. In this case, it makes sense for a company to have a debt offering because it is able to earn a high rate of return on the borrowed funds.

TRY THIS:

When a company can increase its return without increasing its investment, this is known as

a. Debt-to-equity ratio.
b. Leveraging.
c. Good business.
d. Securities trading.

> **HERE'S WHY:**
>
> The correct answer is (b). The relationship of a firm's debt to its equity is expressed in the debt-to-equity ratio. If the company earns a return on the borrowed money greater than the cost of the debt, it is successfully applying the principle of leverage.

Mutual Funds

Mutual funds are often considered as part of an overall investment program. They offer diversification and the expertise of an investment advisory company.

Diversification is a key concept behind mutual funds. By investing in a variety of bonds, stocks, or a mixture of both, you reduce your overall level of risk and smooth out the radical downward and upward movements of individual stocks and bonds. The return on mutual fund shares is generally lower than is that on the stocks and bonds themselves, due to management fees and sales charges, but the risk of capital loss is also less.

Expertise is a second factor behind the growth in mutual funds. An individual investor with limited assets may not have access to highly skilled investment analysts and managers, but by combining assets with those of other small investors in a mutual fund, that skilled professional management is accessed.

Market statistics for the most popular mutual funds are published daily in the financial pages. Figures for small funds and other investment companies, such as publicly traded funds (closed-end companies), specialty funds, and dual-purpose funds, usually appear once a week. The funds are always arranged alphabetically and by management group (see Figure 1-1).

The bid price in the quotation of a mutual fund is identified as its **net asset value** (**NAV**). As is the case with an **OTC** (**over-the-counter**) stock, holders of these shares can usually dispose of them at the bid price by redeeming them rather than selling them to another investor. The offering price is a fixed price dependent on the bid and includes the maximum sales charge used when selling those shares to the investing public. (This sales charge may be subject to discounts for quantity purchasers.) Some offering prices do not have a dollar figure, just the letters "N.L." (no load), indicating that there

MUTUAL FUNDS
Thursday, April 10, 1986

Price ranges for investment companies, as quoted by the National Association of Securities Dealers. NAV stands for net asset value per share; the offering includes net asset value plus maximum sales charge, if any.

	Offer NAV	NAV Price Chg.

AARP Invest Program:

Cap Grw	22.29	N.L.+	.23
Gen Bnd	16.20	N.L.	...
Ginnie M	16.16	N.L.	...
Gro Inc	21.55	N.L.+	.10
TxFr Bd	16.22	N.L.+	.04
TxF Shrt	15.50	N.L.	...

ABT Midwest Funds: .....

Emrg Gr	18.48	20.20+	.30
Growth I	13.42	14.67+	.13
Int Govt	10.82	N.L.+	.01
LG Govt	10.92	11.38+	.01
Sec Inc	11.01	12.03+	.02
Util Inc	15.15	16.57+	.05
Acorn Fnd	40.34	N.L.+	.29
Adtek Fd	12.10	N.L.+	.16

Advest Advantage: ....

Govt	10.11	N.L.	
Growth	10.66	N.L.+	.08
Income	10.42	N.L.+	.03
Specl	10.34	N.L.+	.04
Afuture Fd	14.92	N.L.+	.15

AIM Funds:

Conv Yld	13.33	14.26+	.03
Grnway	10.53	11.26+	.09
HiYld Sc	10.08	10.78+	.01
Summit	7.12	(z) +	.09

Alliance Capital:

Alli Gov	9.44	9.99-	.02
Alli HiY	10.38	10.98+	.01
Alli Intl	20.78	22.71+	.24
Alli Mtge	9.86	10.43	...
Alli Tech	23.24	25.40+	.58
Chem Fd	9.17	10.02+	.11
Surveyr	(z)	(z)	...
Alpha Fd	23.03	25.17+	.24

44 Wall St	4.04	N.L.+	.03
44 WS Eqt	5.80	5.86+	.11

Founders Group Funds:

Growth	9.74	N.L.+	.09
Income	15.39	N.L.+	.08
Mutual	11.12	N.L.+	.13
Special	32.12	N.L.+	.40

FPA Funds:

Capital	13.28	14.43+	.22
New Inc	9.62	10.13+	.01
Paramt	13.90	15.19+	.05
Perennl	18.83	20.58+	.06

Franklin Group:

AGE Fd	3.79	3.95+	.02
Cal TxFr	6.99	7.28	...
Corp Csh	9.38	N.L.	...
D N T C	11.44	12.33+	.14
Equity	6.76	7.29+	.08
Fed TxF	11.67	12.16-	.01
Gold Fnd	7.88	8.50-	.09
Growth	15.19	16.38+	.11
Income	2.26	2.44	...
Ins TxFr	11.67	12.16-	.01
MN Ins	11.70	12.19-	.01
N Y Tax	11.54	12.02-	.05
OHIn TF	11.38	11.85-	.01
Optn Fd	6.28	6.77+	.04
Mich TF	11.35	11.82-	.01
US GvSc	7.51	7.82	...
Utilities	7.90	8.52+	.02

Val Tr	30.47	N.L.+	.27

Lehman Group: ....

Captl	(z)	(z)	...
Invst	(z)	(z)	...
Opprt	(z)	(z)	...
Leverage	8.63	N.L.+	.07

Lexington Group:

CpLdr fr	14.89	15.95+	.06
Gold Fd	3.68	N.L.-	.01
Gnma	8.11	N.L.+	.01
Growth	11.30	N.L.+	.08
Resrch	18.91	N.L.+	.14

Liberty Family Fds: ......

Am Lead	13.58	N.L.+	.12
Tax Free	10.47	N.L.-	.01
US Gvt S	8.81	N.L.+	.01
Ltd Term	12.75	13.11-	.01
Lndner Dv	24.53	N.L.+	.06
Lindner Fd	20.62	N.L.+	.06
LMH Fund	28.18	N.L.+	.11

Loomis Sayles Funds:

Cap Dev	24.14	N.L.+	.51
Mutual	23.61	N.L.+	.28

Lord Abbett:

Affilatd	11.20	12.08+	.13
Bnd Deb	10.96	11.98+	.04
Devl Gro	8.77	9.58+	.12
Govt S	3.36	3.60+	.01
TxF Natl	10.82	11.36	...
TxFr NY	10.99	11.54	...

Monday through Friday *The Wall Street Journal* and other financial publications list mutual funds' net asset values, offering prices, and net asset value changes from the market closings of the previous day. (A "Z" means that no quotation is available.)

Net Asset Value (NAV). Net asset value (NAV) is the intrinsic, or actual, value of a mutual fund's common stock that is based on stock prices at the close of trading. The NAV is computed once a day. The closing price of each stock in the fund's portfolio is multiplied by the number of shares held by the fund. Then the dollar value of each security in the portfolio is totaled, and the fund's debts and liabilities are subtracted. The net sum is divided by the number of shares outstanding. The result is the net asset value of the fund per share.

Example: In the quotations shown, the "Growth" fund under "Founders Group Funds" has a net asset value of 9.74 (that is, $9.74 per share). (The four funds listed under "Founders Group Funds" make up a family, with Founders as the sponsor.)

The net asset value per share now becomes the bid price of a mutual fund's share of stock, and it will change daily as the assets (i.e., the securities owned by the fund) change in value.

For a no-load fund, the NAV is both the bid and the offer—that is, the purchase and redemption price of the fund. For a fund that employs a load (a sales charge), the purchase price is the NAV plus the load. At redemption, it is only the NAV.

NAV Change. Any change in mutual funds quotations is measured from close to close.

Example: In the Founders Group Growth Fund, the change in net asset value from the previous day was +0.09 (that is, up nine cents). (Notice that the NAV is quoted in dollars and cents, not in eighths.)

Offering Price. The offering price is the net asset value plus the sales charge (if any). To figure the amount of the sales charge, simply subtract the net asset value from the offering price. For a no-load fund, the net asset value and offering price are the same.

FIGURE 1-1.   Mutual Fund Quotations.

is no sales charge for the fund, and the offering price is the same as the bid price.

Closed-end funds issue shares of stock once—perhaps more than once if permitted by their charter. They do not issue and redeem shares on an ongoing basis, as do mutual funds. Closed-end stock therefore trades like the stock of any other corporation—it is issued once (in a primary distribution) and then traded (in the secondary market). The bid-asked quotation for a closed-end fund stock has no direct connection to net asset value. In fact most closed-end funds' stock trades at a discount from net asset value.

Commodities/Futures

When someone speaks of commodities, wheat, corn, soybeans, and other farm products may come to mind. Commodities also include such things as gold, silver, platinum, and even lumber and heating oil, to name just a few.

Originally, farmers simply sold their crops as they were harvested and had to be content with whatever they earned from their labors. Some of the nation's produce is still sold on this basis in the cash (actual) market.

However, when people speak of commodities as investment vehicles, they are referring to commodity **future contracts**. Large grain dealers and end users of grain products (for example, food processors and manufacturers) use future contracts to assure themselves of a given supply of a particular commodity on a specified future date at a fixed price. Many of the nation's farmers liked the idea of selling their crops ahead of harvest time at a given price. Commodity future contracts came into being as a third type of participant—investors and speculators—entered the marketplace created by farmers and grain dealers and provided liquidity.

To understand what commodity future contracts represent you must understand that a contract gives the holder the right to buy or sell a given amount of a specific commodity at a set price on a fixed date. A contract represents only the right to buy or sell—it does not represent ownership. For example, if you as an investor feel that a certain commodity will rise in price in the future, you would "go long" a future contract, that is, purchase a future contract that entitles you to buy the commodity in question at a set price on a fixed day. If you feel that a certain commodity will decline in price in the future, you would "go short" a future contract, that is, purchase a future contract that entitles you to sell the commodity in question at a set price on a fixed day.

Because an active market exists for them, commodity future contracts are a liquid form of investment. Beginning with the formation of the Chicago Board of Trade (CBT), the marketplace for future contracts has continued to expand and now includes more than 11 exchanges around the country as well as trading locations in the major financial centers of the world. Likewise, future contracts have developed far beyond the original commodity categories and include such things as financial futures, that is, Treasury bills, bonds, currencies, and Ginnie Maes.

Although future contracts get a plus for their liquidity, you should be aware that they carry a high degree of risk. The risk exists because weather and world conditions are unpredictable and can lead to either an excess of a commodity or a shortage of it. Radical price movements in future contracts is the norm rather than the exception.

Options

Options are another of the newer and more interesting investment vehicles. The buyer of an option obtains, for a limited period of time, the right to either buy or sell 100 shares of a company's common stock at a fixed price. However, an option does not confer ownership, merely the ability to control a specified number of shares for a designated period of time.

Option contracts are of two basic types. The buyer of a **call** option has the right to call (acquire) 100 shares of a company's common stock at a specified price for a limited period of time. The buyer of a **put** option has the right to put (sell) 100 shares of a company's common stock at a specified price for a limited time. If you believe that the price of a company's common stock will rise in the future, you would want to buy call options because calls give you the right to purchase the stock in the future (when you expect it to be selling at a higher price) at today's lower price. Conversely, if you believe that the price of a company's common stock will decline in the future, you would want to buy put options because puts give you the right to sell the stock in the future (when you expect it to be selling at a lower price) at today's higher price.

TRY THIS:

An instrument that gives its owner the privilege of buying an underlying security any time during the instrument's life is a
a. Stock.
b. Bond.
c. Call option.
d. Put option.

HERE'S WHY:

The correct answer is (c). As long as the security is purchased before the option's expiration date and at the price set forth in the contract, then the call option can be exercised.

The concept of leverage is at the cornerstone of the development of options as an investment vehicle. It would cost you $3,000 to acquire 100 shares of a stock selling at $30 per share ($30 per share times 100 shares), but for that same $3,000 you might be able to purchase 10 call options that are selling for $300 each. This type of transaction would allow you to purchase 1,000 shares for a specified time (typically three to nine months) at a specified price per share (typically the price of the stock at the time you buy the option). Before you run out and buy options though, be aware that if you have not exercised your option by the date specified in the contract (referred to as the expiration date), the contract loses all its value and any money you committed to the investment is lost. When you purchase an option you are gambling that your prediction—whether for a rise or a decline in the stock's price—will occur within the time specified in the option contract.

Options are traded on the Chicago Board of Options Exchange (CBOE) as well as on most of the leading stock exchanges; thus options are among the most liquid investment vehicles. But as we in-

dicated in the preceding paragraph, investments in options carry a
high degree of risk and should be approached with caution.

Special Characteristics of Debt Offerings

A debt offering is most commonly found in the form of a bond, or
other instrument of indebtedness. The bond indenture contains a description of the key elements of any bond. For example, the indenture describes what items, if any, of the company's plant or equipment will secure the bond; which bank will act as trustee to represent
the interests of the bondholders; what authority the trustee has to
force the company into bankruptcy if it fails to comply with the terms
contained in the indenture; what rate of interest will be paid to the
bondholders; and how the payments will be made. Rather than examine the indenture itself, most investors rely on their financial ad-
visers to inform them about the terms it contains. Only in the event
of a default do bondholders focus their attention on the indenture
(although many bonds sold and traded today are **debentures,** secured
only by the "full faith and credit" of the borrower rather than by a
particular asset of the company). (See Figure 1-2.)

TRY THIS:

A bond backed by the company's good name is
a. A sinking fund.
b. A debenture.
c. An indenture.
d. An income bond.

HERE'S WHY:

The correct answer is (b). A debenture is an unsecured debt offering by
a corporation, promising only the general assets as protection for creditors. Sometimes the so-called "general assets" consist only of goodwill
and reputation.

FIGURE 1-2a. Bond Certificate (front).

W. R. GRACE & CO.
12⅞% NOTE DUE 1990

This Note is one of a duly authorized issue of Notes of the Company designated as its 12⅞% Notes Due 1990 (herein called the "Notes"), limited (except as otherwise provided in the Indenture referred to below) in aggregate principal amount to $100,000,000, issued and to be issued under an indenture (herein called the "Indenture") dated as of September 15, 1980 between the Company and Bankers Trust Company, Trustee (herein called the "Trustee", which term includes any successor trustee under the Indenture), to which Indenture and all indentures supplemental thereto reference is hereby made for a statement of the respective rights thereunder of the Company, the Trustee and the Holders of the Notes, and the terms upon which the Notes are, and are to be, authenticated and delivered.

The Notes are subject to redemption, upon not less than 30 nor more than 60 days' notice by first-class mail, at any time on or after September 15, 1986, as a whole or from time to time in part, at the election of the Company, at a Redemption Price equal to 100% of their principal amount, together with accrued interest to the Redemption Date (but interest instalments whose Stated Maturity is on or prior to the Redemption Date will be payable to the Holders of such Notes, or one or more Predecessor Notes, of record at the close of business on the relevant Record Date referred to on the face hereof), all as provided in the Indenture.

In the event of redemption of this Note in part only, a new Note or Notes for the unredeemed portion hereof shall be issued in the name of the Holder hereof upon the cancellation hereof.

If an Event of Default, as defined in the Indenture, shall occur and be continuing, the principal of all the Notes may be declared due and payable in the manner and with the effect provided in the Indenture.

The Indenture permits, with certain exceptions as therein provided, the amendment thereof and the modification of the rights and obligations of the Company and the rights of the Holders of the Notes under the Indenture at any time by the Company and the Trustee with the consent of the Holders of 66⅔% in aggregate principal amount of the Notes at the time Outstanding, as defined in the Indenture. The Indenture also contains provisions permitting the Holders of specified percentages in aggregate principal amount of the Notes at the time Outstanding, as defined in the Indenture, on behalf of the Holders of all the Notes, to waive compliance by the Company with certain provisions of the Indenture and certain past defaults under the Indenture and their consequences. Any such consent or waiver by the Holder of this Note shall be conclusive and binding upon such Holder and upon all future Holders of this Note and of any Note issued upon the transfer hereof or in exchange herefor or in lieu hereof whether or not notation of such consent or waiver is made upon this Note.

No reference herein to the Indenture and no provision of this Note or of the Indenture shall alter or impair the obligation of the Company, which is absolute and unconditional, to pay the principal of and interest on this Note at the times, places, and rate, and in the coin or currency, herein prescribed.

As provided in the Indenture and subject to certain limitations therein set forth, this Note is transferable on the Note Register of the Company, upon surrender of this Note for registration of transfer at the office or agency of the Company in the Borough of Manhattan, The City of New York, duly endorsed by, or accompanied by a written instrument of transfer in form satisfactory to the Company and the Note Registrar duly executed by, the Holder hereof or his attorney duly authorized in writing, and thereupon one or more new Notes, of authorized denominations and for the same aggregate principal amount, will be issued to the designated transferee or transferees.

The Notes are issuable only in registered form without coupons in denominations of $1,000 and any integral multiple thereof. As provided in the Indenture and subject to certain limitations therein set forth, Notes are exchangeable for a like aggregate principal amount of Notes of a different authorized denomination, as requested by the Holder surrendering the same.

No service charge shall be made for any such transfer or exchange, but the Company may require payment of a sum sufficient to cover any tax or other governmental charge payable in connection therewith.

The Company, the Trustee and any agent of the Company or the Trustee may treat the Person in whose name this Note is registered as the owner hereof for all purposes, whether or not this Note be overdue, and neither the Company, the Trustee nor any such agent shall be affected by notice to the contrary.

The Notes are hereby designated as Superior Indebtedness for the purposes of (a) the Indenture covering the Company's 4¼% Convertible Subordinate Debentures Due March 1, 1990 issued pursuant to the Indenture dated as of March 1, 1965 between the Company and Chemical Bank New York Trust Company, Trustee, within the meaning of, and as defined in, Section 3.01 of such Indenture and (b) the Indenture covering the Company's 6½% Convertible Subordinate Debentures Due 1996 issued pursuant to the Indenture dated as of November 15, 1971 between the Company and The Chase Manhattan Bank (National Association), Trustee, within the meaning of, and as defined in, Section 3.01 of such Indenture.

Terms used herein which are defined in the Indenture shall have the respective meanings assigned thereto in the Indenture.

ABBREVIATIONS

The following abbreviations, when used in the inscription on the face of this Note, shall be construed as though they were written out in full according to applicable laws or regulations:

TEN COM—as tenants in common
TEN ENT—as tenants by the entireties
JT TEN —as joint tenants with right of survivorship and not as tenants in common

UNIF GIFT MIN ACT—........ Custodian.........
                              (Cust)   (Minor)
              under Uniform Gifts to Minors
              Act...................
                              (State)

Additional abbreviations may also be used though not in the above list.

FOR VALUE RECEIVED, the undersigned hereby sells, assigns and transfers unto

PLEASE INSERT SOCIAL SECURITY OR OTHER
IDENTIFYING NUMBER OF ASSIGNEE

PLEASE PRINT OR TYPEWRITE NAME AND ADDRESS OF ASSIGNEE

the within Note of W. R. GRACE & CO. and does hereby irrevocably constitute and appoint

_____Attorney
to transfer the said Note on the books of the within-named Corporation, with full power of substitution in the premises.

Dated_____

FIGURE 1-2b. Bond Certificate (back).

Bonds used to be issued in two forms—bearer and registered. Bearer bonds are easily transferable from one individual or institution to any other individual or institution because the company assumes no responsibility for identifying or keeping track of the owners of its bonds. But in recent years, only registered bonds have been issued due to governmental pressure to identify the holders of financial assets so that the income derived from these sources can be taxed. Registered bonds oblige the company to identify its bondholders, to pay to the registered owners all interest payments as they come due, and to advise the registered owners of any upcoming developments, such as redemption calls (the retirement of the bond by repayment of the face value or above to the holder).

TRY THIS:

True or False? For a fully registered bond, the name of the owner is maintained by a corporate register.

HERE'S WHY:

This statement is True.

Par Value

Most bonds are issued in denominations of $1,000, and a bond selling at $1,000 is referred to as selling at **par**. The bond tables in the financial press would list a bond selling at par, or $1,000, as 100 (100% of its face value). A bond selling at $1,200 (at a **premium** above par) would be shown as 120. A bond selling at $780 (below par or at a **discount**) would be shown as 78. As with stock, corporate bonds trade at fractional prices in increments of eighths. Bonds issued by the federal government trade in a similar manner, but the increments are expressed in thirty-seconds. For example, a government bond listed a 80.12 means $80^{12}/_{32}$, which translates into $80^{3}/_{8}$, or $803.75.

Ratings

Bonds are given ratings by investors' services such as Moody's and Standard & Poor's. The rating assigned can play a crucial role in determining both the price at which the bond sells and its marketability. The rating of **Aaa** is the highest grade assigned by Moody's and indicates that the company selling the bond has an extremely strong capacity to pay principal and interest. At the other extreme, if a bond is rated by Moody's as **D**, the issuer is in default of the principal and/or interest payments. The rating scale utilized by Standard & Poor's is similar, and both services generally track each other. Ratings are important because few investors have the time or the capability to arrive at their own conclusions about a company's ability to meet its financial commitments. Investors look to the rating services to perform this function. Further, many institutional investors, particularly pension funds and bank trust departments, are prevented by law or policy from investing in bonds rated below the **Baa** category. Thus, low-rated bonds are cut off from a major segment of the bond-investing community.

Call and Sinking Fund Features

As an investor, you should be aware of call and sinking fund features of bond offerings, because such features can have a significant impact on the total return (capital gains or losses plus interest).

A **call feature** requires a company seeking to refinance its debt, that is, "call" its bonds, to pay its bondholders not only principal and accrued interest, but also a premium. In the early years of a bond's existence, this sum can be fairly substantial. From the investor's point of view, a call on bonds means the forced reinvestment of money at a time when interest rates have declined from previous levels; for this reason the call feature provides for the payment of a premium over the face value of the bond, although the premium usually declines over the years.

Not all bond offerings have a call feature. To determine if a particular bond has such a feature, examine the bond's indenture or consult one of the standard reference sources such as Moody's or Standard & Poor's. Through their bond-buying patterns, investors have increasingly indicated that they prefer bonds without call features. This preference is principally a reaction to the volatile interest rates of recent years: many investors saw high-yielding bonds "called away" from them as interest rates declined; in some instances they suffered a loss on their investments. If you own bonds in registered form, you will receive notice of any impending calls, but if the bonds are held in bearer form, you or your financial adviser must keep track of calls through the financial press and publications.

TRY THIS:

A bond is said to have call protection for 10 years. This means
a. The issue may be called any time from issue date up to a maximum of 10 years but may not be called thereafter.
b. The bond may not be redeemed prior to 10 years from issuance.
c. First sinking fund payments begin in 10 years.
d. The interest rate on the bond may not be changed prior to 10 years from issuance.

HERE'S WHY:

The correct answer is (b). Not many investors would commit money to a bond with a high current coupon rate if there were the likelihood of a call to redeem the bonds as soon as interest rates went down and the bonds could be refunded at lower rates. Consequently, protection against such a call for a minimum of 10 years has been a standard practice to assure marketability of longer-maturity bonds.

In the past, bond investors placed an emphasis on whether or not a particular bond had a **sinking fund** feature attached to it. A sinking fund provision means that the company is required to allocate a specific amount of its current earnings toward **retiring** the bond, that is, pay off a given amount of the bond each year. Investors like the sinking fund because it gives them some assurance that the company is working off its debt loan from current earnings rather than waiting until the bonds come due to meet its commitments. Such a provision also has an impact on the issue's market price. Because the company is under an obligation to retire a portion of its bonds on an annual basis, a floor is created for the price of the bond. Such demand by the company for its own bonds tends to smooth out adverse changes in interest rates and the bond market in general and provides greater asset protection for the remaining bondholders.

In recent years, however, most investors have placed less emphasis on the sinking fund feature and more emphasis on the company's earnings and cash flow—the company's ability to service its debt. The rating services also have shifted their emphasis, focusing more on the ability of the company to service its debt and to show earnings and positive cash flow and less on the terms of the indenture itself.

As you can see, there are many different ways of investing and many different markets—some simple, others more complex. The variety of investments available in the fixed income investments market, however, will provide you with plenty of investment alternatives.

2
The Array
of Fixed Income
Products

There are many different kinds of fixed income instruments, the majority of which are discussed throughout this book. However, a brief synopsis of these products is presented in this chapter, beginning with an equity product that has many of the attributes of a debt instrument.

Preferred Stock

Preferred stock is a type of equity investment that first became popular during the 1920s and 1930s. It is a hybrid form of equity investment possessing some characteristics of common stock and some of bonds.

As an investor, you should understand the important characteristics of preferred stocks. Preferred stock represents equity ownership in a corporation, but to a limited degree. Preferred stockholders have no voice in selecting a company's officers and directors, but owners of preferred stocks are guaranteed a fixed dividend payment that takes precedence over any dividend payment to common stockholders. Preferred stockholders also have a more senior claim on the company's assets in the event of liquidation or bankruptcy. Only bond-holders (and other creditors) come before preferred stockholders in such cases.

The Dividend

The issuance of preferred stock is just another way of attracting investors to a company. The primary appeal of preferred stock is the fixed **dividend** that must be paid before any payment is made to common stockholders. This fixed annual dividend is frequently expressed in dollars per share or as a percentage of par value, but the percentage yield varies according to the stock's market price.

EXAMPLE:

A 5% dividend on a preferred stock with a $100 par value translates into a $5 annual dividend (5% of 100). Should the market value of the stock increase to, say, $110, then the percentage of this yield goes down to 4.55 percent ($5 divided by $110). On the other hand, if the market price declines to $90, the yield increases to 5.56%.

TRY THIS:

An investor purchases 100 preferred shares at 80. Their par value is $100, and their dividend is 8%. The investor receives
  I. $800 per year.
 II. $640 per year.
III. 8% yield.
IV. 10% yield.

a. I and III.
b. I and IV.
c. II and III.
d. II and IV.

HERE'S WHY:

The correct answer is (b). On an 8% dividend, the annual yield is $8; multiply that by the number of shares (100) and you obtain the amount the investor receives: $8 \times 100 = 800$. The yield is the dividend divided by the price, or $8 \div 80 = 10\%$.

Priority of Claim

In liquidation proceedings, preferred stockholders' claims to corporation assets have priority over the claims of common stockholders. The preferred holder's claim on the assets of a corporation in dissolution typically consists of

1. The par value.
2. Any dividends in arrears.
3. The pro-rata dividends from the last payment date.

These days, however, the dividend alone does not attract investors. Further concessions and privileges are necessary for a successful offering of preferred shares.

In spite of the apparent advantages of senior claims to dividends and company assets, preferred stocks also have some negative features that you should recognize. While the common stockholder can look forward to dividend increases as the fortunes of the company improve and to possible stock dividends or stock splits, preferred stockholders generally do not enjoy any of the benefits of growth and expansion. Because investors typically look to preferred stock for current income rather than for growth (capital gains), they are particularly concerned about the dividends paid on such stocks. Hence, any increase in the prevailing interest rate has a greater impact on the price of preferred stocks than common stocks.

For the knowledgeable and astute investor, cumulative preferred stock and convertible preferred stock offer the possibility of significant capital gains. **Cumulative preferred** simply means that the dividend accumulates and becomes a debt of the company in those years in which the company is unable to pay the preferred dividend. Also, no dividend can be paid on the company's common stock while the preferred dividend is owed. For the shrewd investor who recognizes a turn-around in the company's business, the purchase of the cumulative preferred stock with a substantial dividend owed may represent a potential windfall profit when the company "cleans up" all the outstanding preferred dividends before resuming payment of dividends on its common stock.

Cumulative preferred stock permits a stockholder to lay claim to any dividends that were omitted by the corporation in previous years. "Cumulative," as we mentioned, means that any unpaid dividends will accumulate, and that this arrearage must be paid in full before any distribution of earnings is permitted to the common stockholder. "Noncumulative" means, of course, that this arrearage need not be paid. Almost all preferred issues are cumulative.

Convertible preferred stock (preferred stock that is convertible into common stock) can also offer special opportunities to the knowledgeable investor. An investor who feels that some time may pass before a company achieves recognition in the marketplace as a "growth" company may purchase convertible preferred stock if the company has such an issue outstanding. By purchasing convertible preferred, the investor is assured of a fixed dividend payment while providing the option of converting from preferred to common stock if and when the company is recognized in the marketplace and its common stock appreciates. Generally, convertible preferreds are more volatile than straight preferreds because their price is affected by the market performance of the common stock to which they can be converted.

Convertible preferred stock enables the holders to exchange their shares for a predetermined number of shares of common stock any time they choose. The corporation sets the terms of a stock's convertibility at the time it makes the initial offering. This sort of preferred stock may be convertible into, say, 2 shares of common stock, into 3.3 shares, or into any other number of shares determined by the issuing company. The ratio of underlying common shares to each share of convertible preferred is called the **conversion ratio**.

Convertible preferred stock represents an interest in the total equity of the issuing corporation—as represented by the company's common stock. If the corporation issues more common stock, the equity interest of convertible preferred stockholders would be diminished. In effect, they would be left holding the same-sized "piece" of a pie that has grown larger by the issuance of additional common shares. So, to protect their equity interest when the company issues more common shares, the corporation invariably guarantees that these holders will be entitled to a proportionately larger number of common shares. Hence they maintain the same percentage of underlying ownership.

Conversion Price

To avoid unwieldy fractions, sometimes extending to five or six decimal places, some corporations express convertibility in terms of a conversion price. The conversion price is a market value level for underlying common stock at which the preferred holder may find it attractive to convert.

The initial conversion price is often set from 15 to 25% above the prevailing market price of the common stock at the time of a preferred stock offering. The conversion price indirectly reveals the conversion ratio of that issue too. When divided into the par value of each preferred share, the conversion price discloses the number of common shares receivable upon exchange. The formula for determining the conversion ratio is

$$\text{Conversion ratio} = \frac{\text{Par value}}{\text{Conversion price}}$$

EXAMPLE:

A convertible preferred stock has a $100.00 par value and a $40.50 conversion price. Its conversion ratio is calculated as follows:

$$\text{Conversion ratio} = \frac{\text{Par value}}{\text{Conversion price}}$$

$$= \frac{\$100.00}{\$40.50}$$

$$= 2.4691$$

That is, each preferred share can be converted into 2.4691 shares of common.

But, let's assume that, with the common stock trading at $36 market price, the company directors vote to split the common stock 2 for 1. That's great for the common stockholders, but it "dilutes" the benefits of the preferred stock's conversion feature. Hence the company directors vote also to halve the conversion price of the preferred stock, from $40.50 to $20.25. Why?

In an "efficient" marketplace, the market price of the common stock will adjust downward to accommodate the split. The trading price will work its way down to a level where twice the number of common shares will be worth what the old shares were worth. Specifically, if 100 shares were worth $3,600 (100 × $36), then 200 shares should be worth $3,600 after the split (200 × $18). Correspondingly, the preferred stockholder's conversion ratio must go up (the holder gets more common shares per preferred share), and the conversion price must go down (to reflect the lower price of the common).

TRY THIS:

A company is in arrears in the payment of dividends. Before paying dividends to the common shareholders, dividends must first be paid to
a. Rights holders.
b. Warrant holders.
c. Cumulative preferred holders.
d. Nonvoting common holders.

HERE'S WHY:

The correct answer is (c). Preferred stockholders are guaranteed a fixed dividend payment that takes precedence over any dividend payment to common stockholders, and they also enjoy a senior claim on any assets in the event of liquidation or bankruptcy.

Participating Preferred

This kind of stock offers the privilege of receiving extra dividends, if declared by the directors of a corporation. After all preferred stockholders (including participating stockholders) receive their usual fixed dividend and after all the common stockholders are paid their previously determined normal dividend, then any additional distributions must include the **participating preferred** stockholders as well as the common stockholders. Almost no participating preferred is outstanding; the same effect can be achieved by issuing convertible preferred shares.

Prior Preferred

Prior preferred stock, also called "preference stock" or "preferred preferred," generally refers to a seniority of one preferred stock over another with respect to the receipt of dividends and/or to a claim upon the assets of the corporation in the event of dissolution. Prior preferred stock is rarely issued.

Callable Preferred

Callable preferred stock permits the corporation to retire the issue, at its option, by paying these preferred stockholders a specified value for their shares. If it recalls the stock in the first few days after issuance, the corporation usually pays them a small premium for their

TABLE 2-1.   Five Types of Preferred Stock.

Type of Stock	Characteristics
Cumulative preferred	Claims previously deferred dividends before common stock can share in profits
Participating preferred	Can receive extra dividends beyond fixed amount
Convertible preferred	Can exchange shares for common stock
Prior preferred	Claims seniority over other preferred stocks in payment of dividends or in distribution of assets if the corporation goes out of business
Callable preferred	Gets premium price if stock is redeemed soon after issuance otherwise, only pay value if company retires it

inconvenience. But the size of the premium declines over time until finally, after about 9 or 10 years, these preferred holders receive only the face value of their certificates (par value) upon recall.

TRY THIS:

If a corporation and its investment banker believe that the price of the company's common stock is likely to rise over time, what may they offer?
a. A callable issue.
b. A convertible preferred.
c. A cumulative preferred.
d. A cash dividend.

HERE'S WHY:

The correct answer is (b). If and when a company is recognized in the marketplace, and its common stock appreciates, investors holding convertible preferred stock can cash in on the rise in price and increased stock popularity.

Bonds

You cannot understand bonds and bond pricing without knowing how the Federal Reserve System works and how it affects interest rate levels in the United States.

The Federal Reserve System and the Availability of Credit

The Federal Reserve Board, or "Fed," has an ongoing and major effect on securities in general, and bonds in particular, because of its mandate to regulate the availability of credit in the American economy. It can make funds accessible to the country's banking community in a trickle or a stream, or it can dry up the money sources—at the headwaters, so to speak—thus making lending possible only under the most urgent of circumstances.

What do the Fed's activities mean to the economy, to the investments industry, and to bond prices in particular? The best measure of the economy is the gross national product—the final value of goods and services the nation produces in a year (currently $4.7 trillion). One way GNP is calculated is by multiplying M1 (currency in circulation plus demand deposits) times velocity (the annual turnover rate of M1). It follows, therefore, that the control of M1 controls the economy. Because of this relationship between M1 and the GNP, the Fed attempts to control M1 by adding reserves to or subtracting them from the banking system through its open market operations, discussed in Chapter 3.

Technically, the banking industry is the only entity that can "create" money, typically in the form of loans to make more earning assets. (Banks are essentially in the business of buying and selling money, and hope to make money on the spread between the interest rates—"prices"—at which they buy and sell.) By adding or subtracting reserves, the Fed assists or impedes the banking industry's ability to create money.

When the Fed's policy entails discouraging lending, it raises interest rates at the source of the money supply, and these elevated rates ripple throughout the economy on every level. The couple setting out to buy their first home cannot obtain a mortgage. The prospective buyer of a new car cannot get financing. The new dining room set has to wait until retail credit eases up. A small store owner cannot obtain the capitalization needed to expand. Large corporations order smaller quantities of raw materials—steel, lumber, concrete, and the like—and defer payment to the last moment, just to conserve their existing funds.

Because bonds are essentially loans that are bought and sold, the Fed's activities—to expand or restrict the availability of credit—have an immediate effect on bond prices. When the Fed discourages lending and interest rates rise, bonds with interest rates lower than other competitive rates generally decline in market value. And the prices of other types of securities often react to the higher rates.

The Fed affects interest rates through its monetary policy, implemented by the Federal Reserve Board of Governors. The three key tools of the controlling monetary policy are:

1. Reserve requirements.
2. Discount rate—the cost of borrowing from the federal reserve window.
3. Open market operations.

The Reserve Requirement

How much money is available for lending at any given time? For a bank to lend "money" (which in this country includes checks as well as currency), it must take money in through various types of accounts:

1. *Demand deposits*—such as checking accounts or a loan where the customer may withdraw funds at any time.
2. *Time deposits*—savings accounts where the customer may deposit or withdraw any amount at any time and earn interest on money while on deposit (interest rates are lower than for time deposits).
3. *Time deposits*—such as certificates of deposit where customers commit money to the bank for a designated period of time, earning interest for themselves and allowing the bank to lend that money at higher interest.

In its definition of basic money supply, which it calls **M1**, the Fed includes currency in public circulation plus demand deposits in commercial banks. **M2** consists of M1 plus savings deposits under $100,000, certain overnight bank borrowings in the domestic and Eurodollar market, repurchase agreements between banks and individuals, plus most money market mutual funds. **M3** includes M1 and M2 plus time deposits over $100,000. In other words, each higher M number expands the definition of the money supply.

Not all the money in the banks is available for lending, due to the Fed's **reserve requirement**. To satisfy this requirement, member banks must set aside a certain percentage of their deposits and not loan it out. These deposits may be in cash in the bank's vault or on deposit with the Fed (Fed funds). This requirement has a quickly felt and easily measured effect on how much "money" is available for credit. The reserve requirement varies with the location and size of the bank, as well as with the types of deposit (demand, savings, or time). As a matter of fact, it may range from as much as 22% on demand deposits to as low as 3% on some time deposits.

What is the purpose of this requirement? Basically, it is to meet depositors' demands for currency. If all depositors demand currency (as opposed to checks) as sole payment of debts, the whole banking system would be severely handicapped in its ability to provide credit to its customers. So a successful commercial bank must be able to meet the normal currency needs of its customers. If it cannot do so, it could face a run on the bank, a situation in which an unusual number of depositors demand currency at once.

TRY THIS:

Federal funds are borrowed most frequently by
a. Commercial banks.
b. Life insurance companies.
c. Over-the-counter broker/dealer organizations.
d. Closed-end investment companies.

HERE'S WHY:

The correct answer is (a). Through these banks, a wide variety of other investors and borrowers have easy access to the money contained there.

LET'S TRY ANOTHER ONE:

The term "basic money supply" is generally referred to by the Fed as
a. M1.
b. M2.
c. M3.
d. M4.

HERE'S WHY:

The correct answer is (a). The key word here is "basic." The other number designations consist of the basic supply (M1) as well as other sources of money.

Discount Rate

The discount rate is a relatively flexible rate of interest that District Banks charge members. When the Board of Governors wishes to discourage banks from lending, it raises the discount rate. When it wishes to encourage lending, it lowers the rate, to make relending more profitable for member banks.

Open Market Committee Activities

The Federal Reserve Open Market Committee meets eight times a year to set policy for adding or subtracting reserves from the banking system, either by the purchase or sale of government securities or by financing transactions. As described in Chapter 2, adding or subtracting reserves changes the banks' ability to "create" money. (Remember, banks are the only entity that can "create" money, but the Federal Reserve can and does impact the banks' ability to do so.)

Bonds Versus Stocks

Bonds are debt securities, that is, evidence of debt. And when investors buy bonds, they are actually lending money to issuers. So the debt consists of a loan from investors to bond issuers, who can be business corporations, the U.S. government, or municipalities. In most cases, bondholders expect to receive regular interest payments of a fixed amount for the duration of the loan (that is, for the term of the bond). At the end of the term, at the maturity date, the issuer is obliged to return the loan amount (the principal). The loan is represented by the bond certificate, which spells out these details of the loan.

As we have already mentioned, bonds differ from stocks. While bondholders are creditors—that is, they have loaned money—stockholders are owners. As owners, they are also said to have an equity interest in the company. As owners, they do not necessarily receive periodic dividends, nor are they guaranteed repayment in full of their original capital. In fact, should an issuing firm go bankrupt, creditors (among them, bondholders) have the right to be repaid before owners (stockholders). So bonds (as well as preferred stock) represent a claim that is senior to that of stock.

Characteristics of Bonds

Interest Payments

Since bonds usually carry a specified rate of interest, issuers generally must make regular interest payments to bondholders for as long as the loan is outstanding. These payments are usually made semiannually on either the first or fifteenth of the month.

EXAMPLE:

A $1,000 bond with an 8% interest rate would pay $80 a year to the holder ($1,000 × .08 = $80). This money would likely be paid in two $40 installments, six months apart, and the checks would be received on either the first or fifteenth of the month in which payment is due.

Ready Marketability

As securities, bonds are actively traded in an extremely liquid secondary market. Most bonds, especially those of highly rated corporations and the government, merit great investor confidence and therefore are readily marketable. They are, in all their forms, certainly more liquid than, say, real estate.

Ready Negotiability

Given their marketability, just how easy is it to transfer the ownership of bonds from seller to buyer? In most cases, it is very easy.

Bearer bonds are issued and distributed without registration in the holders' names. No names are imprinted on their faces. The owners simply clip off the attached interest coupons, which are dated, and deposit them in a bank. The issuer honors the coupons just as it would their own checks. Hence, bearer bonds are sometimes called coupon bonds, and they are freely interchangeable among investors. Federal law (enacted in July 1983) no longer permits bearer bonds to be issued, although many are still outstanding from prior years.

Registered bonds, on the other hand, have the names of their owners inscribed on their faces. In addition, the holders' names and addresses are on record with the issuer. So transferring this sort of bond requires some paperwork, but certainly not enough to make their negotiability difficult. In fact, the advantages outweigh the disadvantages because registered bonds, if lost or stolen, can be replaced.

Trust Indenture

The Trust Indenture Act of 1939, which covers public offerings of debt securities, requires that an independent trustee (usually a bank) must be appointed to safeguard the interest of bondholders and to ensure that issuers abide by the terms of the bond agreement. So the terms of the agreement—interest, maturity, payments, collateral, the trustee's name and address, and so on—must all be set down in a trust indenture, sometimes called a deed of trust.

Face Amount

The face amount—that is, the amount of the loan represented by a bond—is its par value. Par is therefore the issuer's principal obligation to the holder for repayment at maturity. Although bonds may be issued for many different face amounts, the face amount is assumed to be $1,000 unless otherwise specified. Bonds are often quoted at a percentage of the face (or par) value. For example, a bond represented at 75 (percent) does not sell for $75 but for 75% of the par value. A $1,000 bond selling at 75 would therefore go for $750; a $10,000 bond at 75 would mean a market price of $7,500.

Retirement

On the date of maturity, issuers pay back the principal amount plus any interest accrued from the last interest date. How do they make sure they have the money on hand? They have several options: refunding, using a sinking fund, an open market purchase, or exercising a call.

Refunding

When issuers don't have enough excess capital on hand to repay bondholders, they often issue new bonds and use the proceeds either to redeem the older bonds or to exercise a call privilege on an outstanding bond. Thus they redeem the bond and fulfill their promise to the bondholder.

Sinking Fund

When companies issue term bonds—that is, bonds with a single maturity date 15 to 30 years in the future—they often establish a sinking fund. This requires that they set aside funds each year for the redemption of the bonds. Thus, when maturity arrives, they have the needed funds.

Open-Market Purchase

If bonds are trading below their face value, issuers often buy back the bonds, thus accomplishing partial retirement.

Exercising a Call

If issuers redeem their bonds prior to maturity via a call, they usually pay somewhat more than face value for inconveniencing bondholders. This call premium may be, say, an extra $20 per bond in the first five years, $10 in the next five years, and nothing thereafter.

TRY THIS:

Which of the following bond terms is not synonymous with the others?
a. Face amount.
b. Par.
c. Price.
d. Principal.

HERE'S WHY:

The correct answer is (c). All the other terms refer to the same aspect of a bond.

LET'S TRY THIS ONE:

The contract between the issuer of a bond and the investor is called
a. Collateral.
b. The debenture.
c. An indenture.
d. Fully registered.

> ## HERE'S WHY:
>
> The correct answer is (c). Not to be confused with debenture (a debt offering by a corporation), indenture is the written agreement between corporation and creditor containing terms of the debt issue such as rate of interest, means of payment, maturity date, and collateral.

Corporate Bonds

Corporations can raise capital in a number of ways. For short periods—that is, for less than five years—they can raise funds through commercial bank loans, promissory notes, or certificates, whether offered publicly or privately. Most banks, however, will not tie up funds in a loan for more than five years, because they are exposed to interest rate risk along with anyone else in the fixed income market. If, for example, a bank extends a loan at 8% for more than five years, what revenues would it lose if interest rates were to rise above 8% during the term of the loan? Its money should be earning greater returns.

To gain the use of capital for more than five years, corporations may turn to sources other than commercial banks. Borrowing from other financial institutions, such as pension funds or insurance companies, is one possibility. Another alternative is distributing stocks or bonds.

Of the two types of securities, bonds offer issuing corporations several advantages over stocks. Issuing stock, or shares of ownership, can weaken the control of the company's founders over decision making and policy setting. Bonds, on the other hand, do not dilute current shareholders' equity.

Bonds are also preferable to bank loans because they provide capital at rates of interest that are generally lower than bank rates. A commercial bank takes deposits from its customers, pays them one rate of interest, and lends the money to, among other clients, corporations in need of capital. When a company sells bonds directly to investors, it effectively cuts out the bank acting as a middleman—and a tier of interest rates. The borrowing process thus becomes more efficient and less expensive.

Bond issues are even more efficient in that the corporation is spared the burden of having to negotiate a separate loan agreement with every potential creditor. Large amounts of capital can be borrowed from hundreds or even thousands of investors through a single, uniform instrument.

U.S. Government Securities

Some of the most influential money decisions in the world are made every day in the U.S. government securities market. Billions upon billions of dollars change hands against a background of staccato, deal-making phone conversations, ringing phones, and chirping automated quotation and trading systems.

Before seeing how trading in this vast market is conducted (as we'll discuss in Chapter 6), we'll first acquaint you with the array of government instruments offered. These fall into three categories:

Treasury securities.

Government agency issues.

Derivative instruments.

From time immemorial, governments have had to borrow money to get by. It's not that they are more profligate than the rest of us; it's just that large masses of people, or their elected representatives, have always found it easier to spend money for the public good than to collect the necessary taxes to pay these expenses. In time past, such lenders and investment bankers as the Rothschilds have financed the public debt privately, and this gave them inordinate political power. Fortunately, the United States has taken a different tack in funding the public debt.

In this country more than any other, evidence of the government's indebtedness has become legal tender, a reservoir of savings, and the basis of the largest securities market in the world. By preserving political stability, and by giving the Federal Reserve the power to oversee the government securities market, the U.S. government has found itself in the enviable position of being regarded as the premier issuer of debt securities, even though it has no demonstrable ability to repay them and no collateral behind them.

For whatever reason, the Treasury is able to issue many billions in new securities every year and refund countless billions more, all at yields below those on the highest-quality corporate securities. With all this issuing to do, the Treasury has had to adopt a regular schedule of auctions, so that the market can prepare itself to absorb each issue in turn. The regular rhythm of Treasury auctions is one of the most important constants in the government securities market.

The Treasury issues a very wide range of securities, maturing from a few days after issue to 30 years. By tradition, Treasury issues are grouped into three classes—bills, notes, and bonds—all of which will be discussed in further detail in Chapter 6.

Municipal Bonds

Municipal bonds are debt securities issued by states, cities, townships, counties, political subdivisions, and U.S. territories. The capital raised by these securities is used to build a new high school, to construct a water purification plant, to extend a state highway through a rural area, to erect a multisport center, and sometimes just to refund old debt. "Munis" provide the finances that fuel growth and that generate income for local government.

In the United States, municipal debt has a history almost as long as that of the country itself. In the 1820s, booming cities needed money to grow, and they raised the needed funds by issuing bonds. By 1843, when the first records were kept, outstanding municipal debt was at $25 million. Spurred by the needs of a (sometimes violently) growing nation—particularly by the building of the railroads and the development of the West—state and local governments issued more and more debt. Only the Panic of 1873 took the momentum away for a few years, and by 1900 the outstanding municipal debt level had reached the $2 billion mark.

In 1913, the introduction of the federal income tax was to have profound effects on just about all aspects of living in America. With respect to municipal bonds, it raised a state's rights question: May the federal government tax income from state and local debt? Two landmark cases of the 1800s had laid the groundwork for a decision in this area: the Supreme Court cases of *McCullock* v. *Maryland* (1895) and *Pollock* v. *Farmer's Loan and Trust Co.* (1895) made states all but immune to interference by the federal government. As a result of these cases, municipal bond debt was completely exempt from federal taxation until the Tax Reform Act of 1986 was passed.

This act distinguishes between municipal bonds issued before August 15, 1986 and those issued after that date (with exceptions, of course). Munis issued prior to this date retain the tax-exempt features that they offered before it. Any municipal issued after this date falls into one of three categories, depending on its purpose:

Public purpose bonds, issued directly by the state or local authority, are used for traditional "municipal" projects such as a new school building or highway improvement program (projects that are clearly the responsibility of government). These munis are tax-exempt.

Private activity bonds, although issued by the state or local government, supply funds for "private" projects, such as a sports arena, shopping mall, or civic center. These bonds are subject to federal taxation, but they may be exempt from state/local taxation in the states in which they are issued.

Nongovernmental purpose bonds raise funds for "nongovernmental" (but not "private") uses, such as housing or student loans. These are tax-exempt, but the Tax Reform Act puts a cap on the amount that a municipality may issue of such bonds, and the interest is treated as a preference item for purposes of the alternative minimum tax.

As a result, the phrase "municipal bonds" is no longer synonymous with the term "tax-exempts." Although a tax-exempt municipal bond's interest payments (usually on a semiannual basis) are exempted from federal taxation, any profit from its purchase or sale is not exempt.

In the spring of 1988, the U.S. Supreme Court held in *South Carolina* v. *Baker* that provisions in the Tax Equity and Fiscal Responsibility Act of 1982 *denying* federal income tax exemption for publicly offered state and local government bonds not issued in registered form *was* constitutional. This ruling repudiated late 19th century interpretations and clearly affirmed the right of Congress to impose federal tax on municipals if it chooses. In other words, federal tax treatment of state and local government bonds is a matter of statutory law, not constitutional principle, and Congress has the power to raise revenues.

Money Market Instruments

Money market instruments, as contrasted with capital notes, bonds, or debentures, are debt securities that are issued and will mature in a relatively short period of time, usually within one year. Banker's acceptances, certificates of deposit, commercial paper, and some government securities fall into this classification. These and others are discussed in more detail in Chapter 7. Because of their size (buying power) and contacts, money market funds can usually obtain higher yields on short-term investments than can individual investors.

Prices of some money market funds are constant at $1 per share—buy at $1, sell at $1—and only the rate of interest fluctuates. The price of some of the funds fluctuates as does the value of the underlying securities in an investor's portfolio. Changes in value can increase or decrease the price, or increase/decrease the yield.

Interest, earned on a daily basis, is either paid to the shareholder or is reinvested at the end of each month. The rate of interest paid fluctuates on a daily basis because a percentage of the short-term investments in the portfolio mature daily and must be reinvested. The new rate may be higher or lower than the rate on the maturing paper, depending on market conditions.

Money market funds provide a profitable short-term or temporary investment because at times the yields are larger than most investors can obtain elsewhere, and the funds can usually be redeemed on one day's notice.

Other Fixed Income Instruments

A variety of other investment instruments include the following:

Zero-coupon bonds, or **stripped securities** (strips), are Treasury notes or bonds which are sold to investors with their coupons "stripped" or detached. Such notes and bonds are especially suitable for long-range goals such as providing for retirement or a child's education because you can determine ahead of time the actual dollars you will receive when the security matures. As an investor, you must report annually the interest you earn on a zero-coupon bond, even though you do not receive it until the bond matures. For this reason, zero-coupon bonds are considered most appropriate for Keogh and IRA accounts.

Mortgage bonds are secured (or collateralized) by a legal claim to specific assets of the issuer, such as real property like a factory. If the company defaults on payments due the bondholders, they have direct claims on the assets pledged.

If the bond indenture states that the agreement is **open-ended**, the company can use the property pledged as collateral for these bonds for *additional* borrowing. Open-end mortgage bonds are normally issued in a series. All issues in the series give the holders the same claim to the common collateral, or equal "seniority"; that is, no holder has "senior" claim over the holder of another bond in the series.

Issues in a series can differ by having varying interest rates and other distinguishing features. One way in which issues differ is that their maturities are usually staggered according to a schedule set forth in the indenture. The issuing company's total long-term capital needs are met with the capital borrowed only as needed, and the debt is paid off in stages instead of in a lump sum.

If the bond is **closed-ended**, the first lender has "senior status," that is, first claim on the mortgaged property. Other loans can still be secured by the same property, but they are junior to the claims of the prior bondholders.

Sometimes, if a company undergoes reorganization or faces bankruptcy, it might ask first bondholders to surrender their preferred status to a new class of creditors willing to lend capital; they, in turn, become senior bondholders. This new issue, called a "prior lien bond," is then regarded as a first mortgage, and the former issues become second mortgages.

TRY THIS:

True or False? An open-ended mortgage issue is one where subsequent issues are equal in all respects to the original issue.

HERE'S WHY:

You're right, this statement is True.

Mortgage-backed passthrough securities are perhaps the most spectacular development in the government securities market since the early 1970s. During the late 1960s the thrift industry (savings banks, savings and loan associations), which had been the primary source of single-family mortgages, was apparently subject to too many pressures and fluctuations to be counted on to supply the necessary funds. With the creation of GNMA (Government National Mortgage Association) in 1968 came an entirely new security, a cross between a publicly traded bond and a single-family mortgage. It was a security, like a note or bond, representing an interest in a pool of mortgages and bearing the guarantee of GNMA. These were called mortgage-backed passthrough securities (MBSs) because they were backed by federally insured single-family mortgages, on which the principal and interest payments were "passed through" to the holder of the security. The actual issuer of the MBS is a mortgage banker, perhaps a small company that the security owner never heard of. The mortgage banker services all the loans in the pool, collecting the individual monthly payments and passing the funds along, minus a servicing fee, 45 days later.

There are currently over 50,000 pools of GNMA passthroughs in existence, representing a principal of over $70 billion. Since these pools are issued by a large number of mortgage bankers, the only thing giving the market any uniformity is the presence of GNMA's guarantee of timely payment of principal and interest, which incorporates the full faith and credit of the Treasury.

Within the first five years of the 1980s, both the Federal Home Loan Mortgage Corporation (FHLMC) and Federal National Mortgage Association (FNMA) began to issue and guarantee MBSs. Theirs, however, are backed by conventional mortgages, and their guarantees do not incorporate the full faith and credit of the Treasury. As one might expect, their securities carry a higher market yield than do GNMAs, and the market is less liquid. Yet both of their markets are growing all the time.

Because of their mortgagelike nature, the market for passthrough securities has some distinct differences from the market for other debt securities. Traditionally, mortgage trades have been done for settlement several months in the future, when the mortgages are available for delivery. Passthrough securities are traded for settlement from a few days to six months in the future, with the vast majority settling from one to three months after the trade.

Derivative Products

One of the characteristics of the fixed income markets since the late 1960s has been a high degree of interest rate volatility. Who is to blame for that volatility has been a subject of endless debate, but the markets have had to adapt to it nonetheless. Along with the volatility have come large budget deficits and a large volume of Treasury securities issues.

The primary dealer community has limited capital with which to distribute this large volume of securities, and that shortage of capital has been exacerbated by the volatility. Clearly, the dealers had somehow to lay off part of their very high risk.

The solution turned out to be derivative products or investment products whose price performance is derived from another instrument. The best known derivative product is financial futures, but the market also developed options, both exchange-traded and over-the-counter. Collectively, derivative products have changed forever the face of the fixed income markets—especially the government securities market.

Financial Futures

The original derivative product in the fixed income markets was a financial futures contract. **Futures contracts**, which have traded for many years in the agricultural arena, are bilateral agreements to make and take delivery of a physical item at some point in the future. Originally, agricultural products traded for future delivery on an over-the-counter basis. However, because of the predictable seasonal nature of agricultural demand and supply, trading for future delivery became larger than trading for immediate delivery. Futures exchanges were founded to bring order to a chaotic marketplace and to standardize the contracts, thereby enabling buyers to unwind their positions without going back to the original sellers.

What worked for wheat and pork bellies would also work for debt securities. In 1970, the Chicago Board of Trade began trading in futures on GNMA passthroughs, and in 1975 the same exchange began trading in futures on Treasury bonds. If the daily trading volume in Treasuries is so much larger than the trading volume in

GNMAs, why was the GNMA contract started first? Simply because there was already a liquid market in GNMA securities for forward delivery, and the CBT wanted to give a new concept every chance to succeed.

Succeed it did, beyond their wildest imaginations. In 1985, the bond futures contract traded a larger volume than any other futures contract, between 100,000 and 200,000 contracts a day. In terms of representative dollar volume, it traded more than any other single exchange-traded instrument. Stock index futures and options, which were introduced in the early 1980s, trade more contracts on a daily basis, but each contract represents only a fraction of the principal, and risk, of the CBT bond contract. Often the liquidity provided by the traders in the CBT bond pit has been essential to the smooth functioning of the bond market itself.

The primary reason for its trading success is that the CBT contract is a proxy for the entire long-term bond market. That is, at expiration, any Treasury bond with more than 20 years to maturity can be delivered in satisfaction of the contract. Obviously, some mechanism was needed to equate, for delivery purposes, all the deliverable issues, with a variety of coupons, maturities, and yields.

The mechanism chosen by the CBT was the creation of an imaginary bond that the futures contract represented: an 8%, 20-year bond. Thus the price at which the futures contract trades is the one at which an 8%, 20-year bond would be delivered when the contract expires. Other coupons and maturities are equated to the imaginary security through the use of conversion factors, which adjust the principal amounts of bonds to be delivered. Bonds with coupons higher than 8% and maturities longer than 20 years have conversion factors higher than 1. When $100,000 is divided by the conversion factor, the deliverable amount of securities is determined, and that amount can be delivered at the futures price.

EXAMPLE:

An 11¼% bond with 29 years and 9 months to maturity has a conversion factor of 1.334. You could deliver $74,962.52 of this security per contract sold ($100,000 divided by 1.334). By itself, that doesn't help us much, but the contract price, multiplied by the conversion factor, gives us the equivalent delivery price for the security. For our 11¼% bond, assuming a futures price of 75½, the equivalent delivery price would be 100.717, or

$100^{23}/_{32}$ (75.5 × 1.334). The equivalent delivery price can be compared to the current price for the security to see if it makes sense to select this security for delivery. Among all the deliverable securities, one is, by this calculation, the *cheapest to deliver,* and that is what the futures contract follows.

The equivalent delivery price and the current price for the security are almost never the same, even for the "cheapest to deliver" security. Why? When bonds can be carried at a profit, the futures price is always lower than the equivalent delivery price, and when the yield curve is inverted, the futures contract is always higher. This phenomenon, called **convergence**, is purely a function of the cost of carry.

Interest Rate Options

If the theory surrounding financial or commodity futures is relatively straightforward, the theory surrounding options is anything but simple. Whereas a futures contract is a bilateral agreement requiring both sides to perform at expiration, an **option** is the right to institute a transaction at any time before expiration. If the buyer and seller of a futures contract share equal status, the buyer of an option has a decidedly better position than the seller.

Not surprisingly then, the option buyer pays the seller a price for that better position. That price, called the **premium**, is a function of several factors:

Strike price: The price at which the option buyer can execute the transaction.

Term: The number of days until the option expires.

Investment yield: The yield to the holder of the security that underlies the option.

Alternative yield: The yield to the holder of an instrument that matures at the same time as the option expires.

Price volatility: The historical or implied volatility of the price of the item that underlies the option.

Based on this information, you can calculate (or buy a computer program to calculate) the "theoretical value" of any option. **Theo-**

retical value is the premium level at which a theoretical investor would be indifferent between owning the option and the equivalent position in the underlying instrument. For a call, or the right to buy the instrument, the equivalent position would be owning the instrument itself. For a put, or the right to sell the instrument, the equivalent position would be short the instrument itself.

TRY THIS:

The instrument that sets the price at which a delivery will take place at a much later date is a
a. Put option.
b. Call option.
c. Future.
d. Corporate bond.

HERE'S WHY:

The correct answer is (c). The key phrase here is "at a much later date"—thus the term "future."

LET'S TRY ANOTHER ONE:

True or False? Option positions that are not traded out or exercised, eventually are renewed.

HERE'S WHY:

This statement is False. Once an option expires, no further transactions can take place on that contract.

3
What Is Yield?

The purchaser of a debt security generally wants to invest capital for one reason—the rate of return earned by this money. A rate of return on capital is commonly referred to as **yield.** The concept of yield has different meanings for different investors, according to their purposes and objectives.

Types of Yield

Although the indenture describes the terms of the loan implied in bond ownership, it says nothing about the value of the security. To know that, you must understand the three basic types of yield.

Coupon (Nominal) Yield

Nominal yield is the annual interest rate percentage payable, specified in the indenture and printed on the face of the bond certificate. It enables purchasers to determine their yearly flow of dollar income. Nominal yield is fixed and not related to market value.

If a bond has a face value of $1,000 and pays interest at a rate of 8%, the coupon, or nominal, yield is 8%. This comes to $80 a year ($1,000 × .08). Because the coupon percentage rate and principal don't change for the term of the loan, the coupon yield doesn't change either.

The nominal yield is a yearly rate that is usually paid in equal installments, semiannually. Thus an 8% nominal yield would require distribution of $40 in interest on the first or fifteenth day of January and July, or March and September, or any other calendar dates designated in the indenture, as long as the payments are separated by six-month intervals.

TRY THIS:

"Rate of return" can best be described as:
a. Leverage.
b. Refunding.
c. Coupon rate.
d. Yield.

HERE'S WHY:

The correct answer is (d). Yield is the percentage return on an investor's money in terms of current prices.

Current Yield

Unless all bonds trade in the marketplace at par value, a study of nominal yield does not permit investors to compare the return on one bond with other bonds issued previously under different rates and money market conditions. This, of course, is unrealistic. To provide a means of comparison contingent upon interest rates and variable fluctuations in price most public investors rely upon calculation of current yield.

The **current yield** gauges the return on an investment by relating the stated interest rate to the actual number of dollars needed to purchase that security. Current yield is calculated by dividing annual interest dollars by the current market price.

$$\frac{\text{Annual interest payment}}{\text{Current market price}} = \text{Current yield (in decimal equivalent)}$$

Suppose you could buy an 8% $1,000 bond for $800. Regardless of what you paid, you are still entitled to the $80 annual interest. Yet the $80 represents a higher *percentage* yield than the 8% coupon rate. Since you paid only $800 (not $1,000) and still receive $80 return a year, the actual yield is 10% ($80 divided by $800). This is the bond's current yield.

Because this bond is selling at less than its face value, it is said to be selling at a **discount.**

The discounted bond would be quoted at "80," which means $800. To translate the quote into a dollar price, simply multiply it by $10. So a quote for 80½ means $805, that is, 80.5 × $10. A quote of 90⅞ would be $908.75, or 90.875 × $10. As you can see, each eighth of a point in a bond quote is equal to $1.25 (whereas an eighth in stock trading is equal to 12.5 cents).

Dollar Values of One-eighth Increments in Bond Quotes.

⅛	$1.25
¼	$2.50
⅜	$3.75
½	$5.00
⅝	$6.25
¾	$7.50
⅞	$8.75

If the bond were selling for more than its face value, it would be trading at a "premium." For example, suppose the 8% bond were selling for $1,100 (110). In that case, the current yield would be 7.3% ($80 ÷ $1,100)—lower than the coupon rate. In general, therefore, discounts mean an increased current yield, and premiums mean a lessened current yield.

Yield to Maturity

Yield to maturity, another way of looking at a bondholder's return on invested capital, is a more sophisticated approach to the subject of yield. It is used by institutional investors and portfolio managers who supervise pools of capital on a long-term, semipermanent basis. It is also used by professional securities traders as an accurate means of identifying the relative worth of a particular bond.

Yield to maturity (YTM) is an average rate of return involving collective consideration of a bond's

1. Interest rate.
2. Current price.
3. Number of years remaining until maturity.

Current yield does not take into account the difference between the purchase price of the bond and the principal repayment at maturity. Someone who pays $800 for a $1,000 bond will receive $1,000—$200 more than the purchase price—at maturity. That $200 of capital appreciation is also considered part of yield and must be included in yield-to-maturity calculations. For instance, let's say the 8% $1,000 bond has five years left to maturity when it is bought for $800. To include the $200 discount in the yield calculation, divide it by the number of years remaining to maturity. There's a rule-of-thumb formula to calculate this yield which is referred to as yield to maturity. (Actually, the formula for yield to maturity is a bit more complicated than the one we're giving you.)

$$\text{Yield to maturity} = \frac{\text{Coupon} + \text{prorated discount}}{(\text{Face value} + \text{purchase price})/2}$$

In this case, the only piece of information not immediately available is the **prorated discount.** To get that, divide the discount by the number of years to maturity: $200 divided by 5 years equals $40 per year. Let's plug the numbers into the formula and work it out:

$$\text{YTM} = \frac{\text{Coupon} + \text{prorated discount}}{(\text{Face value} + \text{purchase price})/2}$$

$$= \frac{\$80 + \$40}{(\$1,000 + \$800)/2}$$

$$= \frac{\$120}{\$900}$$

$$= 13.3\%$$

Thus, this discounted bond has a

Coupon yield of 8% ($80 ÷ $1,000).

Current yield of 10% ($80 ÷ $800).

Yield to maturity of 13.3% ($120 ÷ $900).

The same yield-to-maturity formula can be applied to bonds trading at a premium, with two slight changes.

$$YTM = \frac{Coupon - prorated\ premium}{(Face\ value + purchase\ price)/2}$$

Suppose the same 8% $1,000 bond were selling for $1,100 with five years to maturity:

$$YTM = \frac{Coupon - prorated\ premium}{(Face\ value + purchase\ price)/2}$$

$$YTM = \frac{\$80 - (\$100 \div 5\ years)}{(\$1,000 + \$1,000)/2}$$

$$YTM = \frac{\$80 - \$20}{\$1,050}$$

$$YTM = 5.7\%$$

This bond, selling at a premium, has a

Coupon yield of 8% ($80 ÷ $1,000).

Current yield of 7.3% ($80 ÷ $1,100).

Yield to maturity of 5.7% ($60 ÷ $1,050).

Yield to maturity is generally what bond traders are referring to when they use the word "yield." As we mentioned, of the three, it is the *one* type of yield that assesses the effect of principal, coupon rate, and time to maturity on a bond's actual yield.

TRY THIS:

If the yield to maturity equals the nominal yield on a new municipal offering, then the offering price was:
a. Less than 100.
b. 100.
c. More than 100.
d. Impossible to determine.

HERE'S WHY:

The correct answer is (b), nominal yield is coupon yield. The yield to maturity and nominal yield coincide only when the bond is offered at par. A premium (or discount) would cause the YTM to drop below (or exceed) the coupon rate, respectively, because of the loss (or gain) as the bond price approached its principal amount at maturity.

Total Return

Fluctuating interest rates by far, have the greatest impact on a bond's **total return,** which is the return based on the reinvestment of interest payments over the term to maturity.

Up until the 1950s and 1960s, many bond owners—such as university or foundation endowments—simply took their coupon interest payments and spent them. At that time, many bond certificates were printed with coupons attached, each coupon representing an interest payment. To receive your interest payment on this type of bond, known as a "bearer" bond, you had to cut off a coupon and present it to the issuer, usually through a financial intermediary such as a bank or brokerage firm. This practice, known as **coupon clipping,** became associated with affluent investors, the perception being that the wealthy could afford to buy enough bonds to live off the coupons.

Coupon clipping also reflected a form of simple interest. If a person buys a bond and does not reinvest the coupon payment dollars, then the principal remains constant—whether the price paid for the bond was at face value, a premium, or a discount. The earlier examples of coupon rate and current yield were examples of simple interest because they assumed that the interest was not reinvested.

Once interest dollars are reinvested, however, the bondholder starts receiving **interest-on-interest.**

EXAMPLE:

Suppose a pension fund portfolio manager (PM) has in the fund's holdings 25 $1,000 8% bonds. Every year these bonds earn $2,000 in interest (.08 × $1,000 face value × 25 bonds). With that $2,000, the manager buys two more of the same type of bond. In so doing, the PM has converted the $2,000 interest payment into $2,000 of additional principal—on which interest will be paid. The portfolio now contains $27,000 worth of these bonds, and the following year's interest will be $2,160 ($27,000 × .08). If the $2,160 is used to buy additional bonds, then the next year's principal becomes $29,160. (This example, of course, ignores commissions, other costs, and tax considerations.)

Interest-on-interest is a form of **compounding.** Compound interest can dramatically increase the total return to the bondholder, typically over half of a bond's total compounded return.

EXAMPLE:

Suppose our 8% $1,000 bond were bought for $1,000 (face value) at issuance and held for 20 years to maturity. If the bondholder were to clip coupons for 20 years, the total dollar return would be $1,600 ($80 × 20 years). This would be an example of simple interest. On the other hand, if for that same term the bondholder reinvests all interest payments for a return also of 8%, the return is much greater. Without going into the somewhat complicated math, the additional dollar return over 20 years would be $2,201, for a total compounded return of $3,801 ($1,600 simple interest + $2,201 interest-on-interest).

This is not to say that interest has to be reinvested in the same bond. If other or better investment opportunities present themselves as interest payments are received, all the better. For instance, if the $1,600 in coupon payments were consistently reinvested in an instrument that returned 10%, the total compounded return would be $4,832—$3,232 of that being interest-on-interest.

Understandably, the value of interest-on-interest diminishes with the time left to maturity. In the preceding example, the interest-on-interest for an 8% bond held for 20 years was 58% of the total return: $2,201 of $3,801. If the bond were held for 10 years under the same conditions, the interest-on-interest would represent only 33% of the total compounded return: $800 simple interest + $394 interest-on-interest for a total of $1,194. For five years, the total compounded return is only $482: $400 simple and $82 compound. For one year, the interest-on-interest is only $1.63: 2% of the total compounded return.

As you can see, the total compound return, or "total rate of return," is not the same as yield to maturity. YTM is simply a number that can be calculated from the bond's principal, coupon rate, and time left to maturity. It expresses only the present value of the bond's cash flow. Total return is calculated from principal, coupon rate, and interest-on-interest. It assumes that the coupon dollars will be put to work earning additional dollars. While the dollar yields for the two types of calculations may differ—and usually do—the percentage rates of return may be the same under one or more of the following conditions.

First, suppose the bond has a zero coupon. In other words, the interest is deducted from the face value up front, as in the case of series EE savings bonds. Since no coupon dollars are received, there is no opportunity to reinvest them. In such cases, the yield-to-maturity rate on a zero-coupon bond would be the same as the rate of total return because the interest has, in effect, already been "reinvested" at the YTM rate.

Second, if only one payment period is included in the calculation, then there is no opportunity for reinvestment. This would be the case if you were to make a YTM calculation on a bond with only six months to maturity (that is, one interest payment period). Since there is no opportunity for reinvestment, the two rates are the same.

Third, if all coupons are reinvested at the YTM rate, then it would, of course, equal the rate of total return. Again, the dollar yield for total return would be higher than that for YTM, but the rates would be the same.

Of the two types of return, the rate of total return is generally regarded as a better gauge of market value than yield to maturity for two reasons if income is reinvested.

First, the total rate of return is more realistic in that it takes into account future changes in reinvestment rates. For instance, if future coupons are reinvested at less than the YTM rate, the rate of return will decrease. If future reinvestment rates are higher than YTM, then the rate of total return rises. Yield to maturity accounts for none of this.

Second, it enables investors and traders, given a reasonable assumption about future reinvestment rates, to forecast total return more accurately.

EXAMPLE:

Suppose a portfolio manager expects bond rates to decline over, say, the next year, and she decides to invest some of the portfolio's funds in bonds at an 8% yield to maturity. Given her reinvestment rate assumptions, she knows that the actual total return will be less than 8%, and she can adjust her expectations accordingly.

TRY THIS:

Payment of interest on a bond is made on the same day of the month throughout the life of the instrument. Which notation best illustrates this?
a. F&A 15.
b. F&J 15.
c. A&N 10.
d. J&A 23.

HERE'S WHY:

The correct answer is (a). Remember, interest is usually distributed on the first or fifteenth day of the month, with six months between each payment. F&A 15 stands for the fifteenth day each of February and August.

The Yield Curve

Given an assumption about reinvestment rates, how *do* professional traders and portfolio managers make their buy and sell decisions? What general priniciples do they use with respect to yields, prices, and risk? In brief, their thinking and actions are based on their analysis of what is known as the **yield curve.**

To explain the yield curve and its implications, let's assume that the reinvestment rate will stay fixed at 8% until maturity. Given that assumption, the yield to maturity can be depicted simply in a graph as in Figure 3-1.

The horizontal line extending from the tic mark for 8% represents the anticipated "yield curve" for this bond. (It's called a "curve" even though it's straight in this particular instance.) If the coupons are reinvested consistently at 8% for 20 years, then at maturity the actual yield curve will look just like that line. Also, the actual total rate of return will be the same as the yield to maturity, because all reinvested interest will earn interest at 8%. But what if the coupons were reinvested at different rates of return? As soon as that happens, the line for total rate of return diverges from that for yield to maturity. If the coupon reinvestment rate is higher than the YTM rate, the total rate of return will be higher. Given a lower-than-YTM rate of reinvestment, the total rate of return will be lower. The varying rates of return can be depicted as in Figure 3-2.

In this figure, the line above the one for the anticipated YTM assumes that the bondholder was able to put coupon dollars to work in such a way as to earn a rate greater than 8%. Perhaps he bought

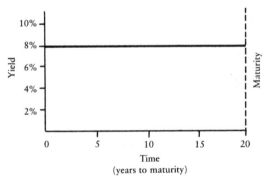

FIGURE 3-1.   Yield to Maturity.

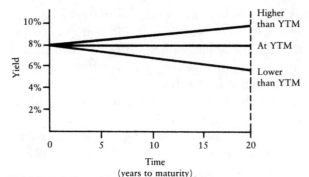

FIGURE 3-2.   Varying Rates of Return.

other bonds or preferred stock with higher YTMs; investing in another investment vehicle does not lessen the compounding effect.

The lower line demonstrates the total rate of return if the bond-holder was unable to reinvest at the YTM rate. Maybe some of the coupons had to be applied toward a downpayment on a car, in which case the yield on those dollars drops to zero. Perhaps some coupon dollars were put into a 5% or 6% certificate of deposit, in anticipation of paying a tuition bill. In such cases, the total rate of return diverges downward from the YTM rate.

The yield curve is therefore a depiction of bond market rates over time. The curve is supposed to represent the net result of all the buying and selling in the market—and therefore reflect the net effect of supply and demand pressures. The curve demonstrates graphically what market participants are willing to pay for short-term, intermediate-term, and long-term debt instruments.

A typical yield curve therefore, looks like that in Figure 3-3.

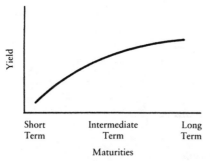

FIGURE 3-3.   Typical Yield Curve.

This graph is known as the "indifference curve," since it shows that the market is collectively "indifferent" to accepting one yield at a given maturity along with a different yield at another maturity. (This coexistence of various yields at different yields is referred to as the "term structure" of rates.)

As an example, let's take the preceding yield curve and assign some value to it (see Figure 3-4).

One-year securities are yielding 7% and two-year securities 8%. The market is indifferent to 7% one-year and 8% two-year instruments in the same market.

That seems strange, but there is a theory that attempts to explain this attitude on the part of investors. The **expectations theory** views the yield curve as a function of buyers' expectations of future interest rates. In our example, the holders of a one-year 7% security are content because they expect rates to increase, thereby enabling them to reinvest at maturity in another one-year security at 9%. Their two-year yield would therefore be

$$7\% \text{ (1 year)} + 9\% \text{ (1 year)} = 8\% \text{ (2 years)}$$

Similarly, holders of the 8% two-year security can hold the instrument till maturity, and then sell it at the expected YTM of 9%. The two-year rate would then be

$$8\% \text{ (2 years)} + 1\% \text{ (1 year)} - 1\% \text{ (1 year)} = 8\% \text{ (2 years)}$$

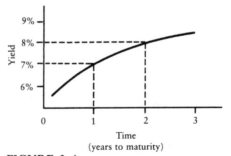

FIGURE 3-4.

Yields on shorter-term securities are generally more volatile than are those on longer-term ones. Given terms to maturity of only several years, changes in price are not drastically amortized and therefore have significant effects on yield to maturity.

An upward-sloping yield (Figure 3-5) reflects higher future rates. The underlying reasoning is that investors tend to sell longer-term securities and buy shorter-term ones. This is another way of saying that they have a greater "liquidity preference." This theory holds that investors attach greater value to shorter-term securities because they are "closer to cash." Looking at it a different way, investors may demand a higher return to invest longer term because there is more uncertainty about future interest rates, creditworthiness of the issuer, economic trends, and the like. The horizontal yield curve has buying pressure (demand) on it short term and selling pressure (supply) long term.

The curve rotates, under the pressures of supply and demand, until market equilibrium is restored. This straight-line yield curve therefore represents the effects of investor's expectations with respect to yield and their collective preference for more liquid, short-term instruments.

But it does not show the effect of investors' assessment of risk. The working principle with respect to risk is that prices become more volatile as the term to maturity increases. Thus, to reflect this, and assuming interest rates are expected to rise, the prices of longer-term securities tend to be lower than those of shorter-term ones. Inasmuch as lower bond prices increase yield to maturity, longer-term maturities are associated with lower prices and higher YTMs.

In addition, changes in price have a lessened effect on longer-term

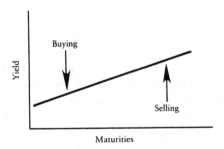

FIGURE 3-5.   Upward-sloping Yield Curve.

yields. For example, a $100 change in the price of a one-year bond affects the yield by the full amount. For a two-year bond, the annual yield is affected by $50. As the term to maturity increases, a price change is more and more amortized, and its effect increasingly diluted. Therefore, prices must change more dramatically on long-term securities to have any significant effect on yield. As a result (the mathematical reasons being set aside), the actual yield curve is indeed a curve (see Figure 3-6).

This is not to say, however, that all yield curves are upward-sloping. The assumption in all our examples has been that rates are expected to be higher for longer-term securities. When future rates are expected to decrease, the yield curve descends. (See Figure 3-7.) In such a case, reinvestment rates and total return are going to decrease.

Yield curve analysis extends far beyond these rudimentary concepts. Professional traders and portfolio managers must understand in complex detail the relationships among price, yield, liquidity, and risk. They must be able to "ride the yield curve," that is, buy and sell debt instruments so as to obtain the greatest total return.

TRY THIS:

The typical scale written on a new 20-year serial issue, assuming normal interest rate conditions, would show yields to maturity
a. Equal for each of the 20 years.
b. Lowest short term, rising gradually to highest long term.
c. Highest short term, declining gradually to lowest long term.
d. Higher short term, lower intermediate term, higher long term.

HERE'S WHY:

The correct answer is (b). Under normal interest rate conditions, shorter maturities have lower yields than longer maturities for the greater exposure to market and purchasing power risks. An inverted scale would be more unusual, featuring higher near-term rates. This happens during extremely tight near-term credit conditions, sometimes called a "credit squeeze" or a "credit crunch."

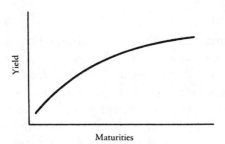

FIGURE 3-6.   Yield Curve.

You can construct your own yield curve today. Take out a newspaper with closing treasury prices. Select yields of issues maturing each year—selling nearest par (100)—out to ten years, then 15-, 20-, and 30-year maturities. Write these down on a piece of paper, then plot the yields on the *y* axis and the maturities on the *x* axis. Draw a curve between the points and you will have constructed the yield curve today.

Factors Affecting Bond Values and Prices

While yield curve analysis enables traders and investors to compare debt securities with different coupon rates and terms to maturity, it does not determine price. Bond prices depend on a number of factors, such as the ability of the issuer to make interest and principal payments and how the bond is collateralized.

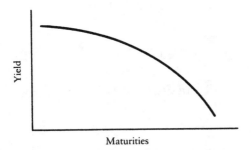

FIGURE 3–7.

Interest Rates

An across-the-board factor that affects bond prices is the level of prevailing interest rates (which is why the Fed plays such a role in bond pricing). In previous examples, an 8% bond yielded different rates depending on whether the bond sold at a premium or discount. What was not explained was *why* the bond should sell for more or less than its face value. The reason has to do with interest rates.

Assume that the 8% bond was issued five years ago, when prevailing interest rates (on similar investment vehicles) were about 8%. Further assume that current prevailing interest rates are up to about 9%. Why should investors buy a five-year-old bond yielding 8% when they can buy a newly issued 9% bond? The only way the holder of an 8% bond can find a buyer is to sell the bond at a discount, so that its yield to maturity is the same as the coupon rate on new issues.

EXAMPLE:

Let's say interest rates increase from 8% to 10%. With 15 years to maturity, an 8% bond has to be priced so that the discount, when amortized over 15 years, has a yield to maturity of 10%. That discount is a little under $200:

$$\text{YTM} = \frac{\text{Coupon rate} + \text{prorated discount}}{(\text{Face value} + \text{purchase price})/2}$$

$$= \frac{\$80 + (\$200 \div 15 \text{ years})}{(\$1,000 + \$800)/2}$$

$$= \frac{\$93.33}{\$900}$$

$$= 10.4\%$$

The 8% bond with 15 years to maturity must sell at a little over $800 to compete with 10% issues.

The possibility that interest rates will cause outstanding bond issues to lose value is called **interest rate risk.**

Yet there is an upside to this risk. If interest rates decline during the five years that the 8% bond is outstanding, the holder could sell it for enough of a premium to make its YTM rate comparable to the lower yields of recent issues.

For instance, should interest rates decline to 7%, the price of the 8% bond with 15 years to maturity will increase by about $100.

$$\text{YTM} = \frac{\text{Coupon} - \text{prorated premium}}{(\text{Face value} + \text{purchase price})/2}$$

$$= \frac{\$80 - (\$100 \div 15)}{(\$1,000 + \$1,100)/2}$$

$$= \frac{\$73.33}{\$1,050}$$

$$= 7.0\%$$

All other influences aside, the general principle is that bond prices tend to increase when interest rates fall and to decline when interest rates rise.

As a corollary, the prices on longer-term bonds fluctuate more than do those of shorter-term bonds in response to interest rate changes. For example, we know that the 8% bond with 15 years to maturity has to adjust nearly $200 in price to accommodate a rise in rates to 10%.

Under the same circumstances, an 8% bond with five years to maturity requires less of a discount—$80 to be exact.

$$\text{YTM} = \frac{\$80 + (\$80 \div 5)}{(\$1,000 + \$920)/2}$$

$$= \frac{\$96}{\$960}$$

$$= 10\%$$

Thus, the shorter the term to maturity, the less volatile the price adjustment to a change in interest rates.

TRY THIS:

True or False? A discount price gives the buyer an increased dollar yield to maturity.

HERE'S WHY:

This statement is true.

The intimate relationship with interest rates is the key to understanding what drives bond prices. When the U.S. Treasury, a municipality, a corporation, or any other issuer decides on a primary offering of bonds, it must weigh, among other things, the effect of interest rates.

When bonds start trading in the "secondary" market (after they are initially brought to market), they are subject to ongoing interest rate risk. That is, bond prices react to the same factors acting on interest rates. These factors are generally recognized to be the following:

The Business Cycle

During an upswing, American businesses start borrowing money to buy equipment or raw materials, to build plants, or to develop new services. Would-be borrowers (the demand side) compete for diminishing funds (the supply), driving the cost of money (interest) up. Banks start raising their lending rates. To attract money into the market, yields have to rise. As a result, the generally accepted principle is that, as economic activity picks up, interest rates tend to rise.

Inflation

When the costs of goods rise, lenders have to increase their rates of interest to offset their loss of purchasing power. Borrowers pay the higher rates because they expect to use the money profitably and pay back the loan with future dollars of reduced purchasing value. Consequently, interest rates are thought to include borrowers' expectations with respect to inflation. Whether or not that assumption is valid, most economists agree that interest rates (the cost of money) rise with the inflation rate.

Flow of Funds

At most brokerage firms, economists analyze how capital is flowing through the economy and try to project the future amount of borrowing. In so doing, they are attempting to gauge the supply side (future borrowing) of interest rates. If their analyses are correct, they may be able to project future interest rates.

When it comes to interest rates and regulating money and credit in the United States, the Federal Reserve System plays a major role. When the amount of available funds is reduced, competition for these monies increases capital borrowing costs. But what about long-term debt, issued under the older and cheaper terms, that has 10, 15, 20, or even 25 years remaining until maturity? Obviously, such a security is no longer as attractive at face value as it was before. This is especially true if lenders can employ their money at higher current rates. Therefore, the older bond with the lower fixed interest rate must invariably decline in value until its yield is comparable to the newly prevailing financial conditions.

Other Factors Influencing Bond Prices

Issuer's Ability to Pay

One or more of the three major rating services gauges a corporation's ability to honor an obligation by assigning to its publicly owned debt a letter rating that indicates its investment quality. These advisory services are:

Fitch Investors Service.

Moody's Investors Service.

Standard & Poor's Corporation.

Each organization examines the corporation's financial statistics and management policies to determine the quality of its debt and then interprets this information according to its own confidential criteria. As a result, it is not unusual to find the same corporate issue carrying a confusing **split rating** (two unequal grades assigned by different services). Nor is it necessarily an adverse reflection on a corporation for its bonds to have no rating at all. Private placements and bonds of corporations in certain industries are often unrated as a result of a particular firm's policy.

In general, an issue's rating hinges upon the following:

1. The corporation's past earnings records.
2. The corporation's current financial position, including
   a. working capital.
   b. the amount of debt outstanding, its maturities, sinking fund provisions, and ranking.
   c. the extent of its tangible assets.
3. The nature of the corporation's business, including
   a. the character of the industry.
   b. the necessity of its product.
   c. the firm's position in the industry.
4. The continuity and consistency of management policies and controls.
5. The corporation's labor relations.

TRY THIS:

Arrange in order the following bond ratings, starting with the lowest:

  I. Baa.
 II. A 1.
III. A.
IV. Aa.
a. II, I, III, IV.
b. IV, I, II, III.
c. I, III, IV, II.
d. I, III, II, IV.

HERE'S WHY:

The correct answer is (d). All are "investment grade" or "bank quality," ranging from "lower medium grade" to "high grade."

Call Feature

The presence of a call feature in the indenture of a bond tends to establish a ceiling for the price of that security. After all, who would buy a bond significantly above its call price knowing that the company can retire it at any time and pay holders only the redemption value specified? In fact, excluding consideration of bonds that are also convertible, the only time a bond trades significantly above face value is when interest rates are declining in the financial community. In such cases, responsible management would probably call that older, more expensive issue anyway and refinance the debt through refunding.

Because of unsettled monetary conditions in recent years, investors have demanded and received "call protection" for the first 5 to 10 years of a bond's lifetime. That is, the bonds are noncallable for the first 5 to 10 years and then become redeemable at declining premium prices as the issue ages toward its maturation date.

TRY THIS:

True or False? The process by which bonds are retired through the issuance of new debt instruments is known as refunding.

HERE'S WHY:

This statement is True.

Sinking Fund

Provisions for a significant "sinker" will also exert an influence upon that issue's market price. When the corporation is obliged to retire a portion of its debt annually through open market purchases or exercise of a call, it provides a flexible floor in the price of that security. This built-in demand partially offsets the effect of adverse changes in the money market and provides more asset protection for the remaining holders of that issue.

Convertible Features

The conversion privilege, while considered to be the prerogative of the bondholder, is also advantageous to the issuing corporation. Because this form of dual status (creditor/stockholder) is an attractive feature for investors, a corporation can issue this obligation with a somewhat lower interest rate than is necessary for ordinary straight-debt securities. Furthermore, if the company prospers, thereby experiencing appreciation in the value of its underlying stock, this debt can be eliminated with a minimal outlay of cash. The corporation merely calls the issue, thus forcing the bondholders to convert into equity or lose the economic advantage of the stock's prevailing market price. That is when the minimal outlay of cash is required. Somewhere between 1% and 5% of all convertible bondholders neglect to act in time to effect the exchange and can subsequently claim only redemption value from the corporation.

TRY THIS:

What has the most influence on income-bearing or fixed dividend securities?
a. Bond prices.
b. Interest rate fluctuations.
c. Dividends.
d. Coupon rates.

HERE'S WHY:

The correct answer is (b). Though there are other influences, the most important one is the effect of interest rates.

4
Corporate Bonds

Corporations can raise capital in a number of ways. For short periods, that is, for less than five years, they can raise funds through commercial bank loans, promissory notes, or certificates, whether offered publicly or privately. Most banks, however, will not tie up funds in a loan for more than five years, because they are exposed to interest rate risk along with anyone else in the fixed income market. If, for example, a bank extends a loan at 8% for more than five years, what revenues would it lose if interest rates were to rise above 8% during the term of the loan? Its money should be earning greater returns.

To gain the use of capital for more than five years, corporations may turn to sources other than commercial banks. Borrowing from other financial institutions, such as pension funds or insurance companies, is one possibility. Another alternative is distributing stocks or bonds.

Of the two types of securities, bonds offer issuing corporations several advantages over stocks. Issuing stock, or shares of ownership, can weaken the control of the company's founders over decision making and policy setting. Bonds, on the other hand, do not dilute current shareholder's equity.

Bonds are also preferable to bank loans because they provide capital at rates of interest that are generally lower than bank rates. A commercial bank takes deposits from its customers, pays them one rate of interest, and lends the money to, among other clients, corporations in need of capital. When a company sells bonds directly to investors, it effectively cuts out the bank acting as a middleman— and a tier of interest rates. The borrowing process thus becomes more efficient and less expensive.

Bond issues are even more efficient in that the corporation is spared the burden of having to negotiate a separate loan agreement with every potential creditor. Large amounts of capital can be borrowed from hundreds or even thousands of investors through a single, uniform instrument.

The Demands of Corporate Leverage

When a corporation borrows money at a fixed rate of interest and uses the money to generate a greater rate of return, this strategy is called **leverage**. The borrowed funds can be used for business expansion, which will theoretically increase the firm's income, or for relending at a higher rate, which will earn revenues on someone else's money. Either way, it is important to hold down the expense of the borrowed money and to keep up the rate of return received.

The relationship of a firm's debt to its equity is often expressed in the debt-to-equity ratio which is the percentage of debt to the total capitalization of the firm. A high debt-to-equity ratio can mean higher profits for the firm in periods of good business, but can mean greater risk in bad times. Minor changes in sales and income can have a sizable impact on the company's profits and its ability to honor debt obligations. This makes leverage a very speculative type of capitalization.

TRY THIS:

Which is an example of leverage?
a. A trader sells common stock short, buys a convertible bond for an equivalent number of shares, converts, and covers the short sale.
b. A company borrows money at 6% and uses the money to earn 10%.
c. An investor simultaneously buys and sells the same security for a quick profit.

d. A corporation redeems its convertible bonds before the maturation date.

HERE'S WHY:

The correct answer is (b). In finance, leverage is the relationship of a firm's debt to its equity, as expressed in the debt-to-equity ratio. If the company earns a return on the borrowed money greater than the cost of the debt, it is successfully applying the principle of leverage.

Corporate Bond Underwriting

Before a bond or security can be issued or offered for the first time to the investing public, it must first go through what is called an **underwriting process.** This is done by the underwriter, an investment banker who serves as a middleman between the corporation and the public. The term "investment banker" can be somewhat misleading because it is really a brokerage firm, not a bank per se, and the firm is not allowed to accept deposits from anyone. Its main purpose is to advise the corporation of the best possible way to bring the bond to market and to help the corporation follow through on the advice given and raise the necessary funds in the form of the bond issue.

There are basically two ways in which the investment banker underwrites a bond. One way is in a **negotiated deal,** where the terms of sale, price, maturity, and interest are discussed and negotiated between the underwriter and the issuing corporation. The other underwriting method is by **competitive bidding,** where the buyers of the issue determine the final price and interest of the bond. Most corporations use the negotiated method of underwriting for their bond issues. (Competitive deals are explained later in connection with municipal securities.)

The Negotiated Offering

The Preliminary Agreement

The first step taken is by the issuing corporation. (See Figure 4-1.) The officers of the company choose an underwriter based on the investment banker's reputation, expertise, abilities in distributing se-

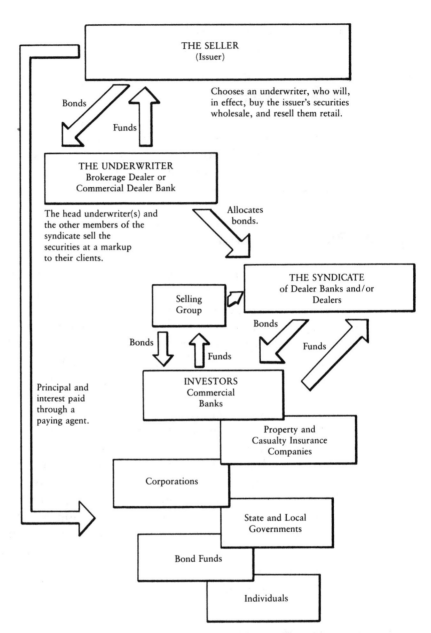

FIGURE 4-1.   The Negotiated Sale Procedure.

curities, capital, and overall organization. If the corporation has issued debt securities before, it is likely to work with the same underwriter in subsequent offerings. Pertinent information about the corporation must be presented to the underwriter's **corporate finance department,** where the information is reviewed. A preliminary study is made with the following information about the corporation outlined: needs, reputation, products, balance sheets, earnings outlook, labor relations, and research expenditures/effectiveness.

The next step is taken by the underwriter. If satisfied that the corporation is healthy enough to stand behind a public offering, then the underwriter sends to the issuer a **letter of intent** summarizing the general terms of the proposed bond issue. The two parties, along with their lawyers, review the proposed terms, discuss the possibilities and alternatives for issuing the bond—what's best for both the corporation and the investor—and agree on the terms to accompany the issue. The exact price and interest rate, however, are not determined until just before or on the actual sale date. The agreed-upon terms constitute the preliminary agreement.

The Syndicate

Once the preliminary terms have been agreed upon, the underwriter usually forms an underwriting group called a **syndicate.** This is a group of brokerage firms that agree to guarantee or underwrite the sale of the new issue. The risk and commitment of capital is spread out among several firms rather than a single underwriter taking on all the responsibility and expense. The underwriter who negotiated the preliminary agreement becomes the **syndicate manager.** As such, the firm is given the authority to negotiate with the issuer on the price of the issue, settle terms on the compensation the syndicate members should receive for the risk they are taking on in distributing the issue, and perform other functions which are explained later in connection with the Agreement among Underwriters.

The first function of the syndicate group is to ensure that a **registration statement** is sent to the Securities and Exchange Commission (SEC). This detailed document outlines such information as the company's business, the purpose of the issue, the type of bond, the approximate amount of the bond, the products and market of the company, and problems the company may be having (such as lawsuits held against them). If the SEC finds serious false statements

on the registration statement after they review it, they can place a
stop order on it which halts the registration process.

The registration statement is necessary because corporate bonds
are subject to the requirements of the Securities Act of 1933. The
thrust of the Act is simple: Unless the law classifies a security as
"exempt," any security sold interstate must be registered with the
SEC before it may be offered publicly. (Tables 4-1 and 4-2 list exempted securities and transactions.) Although the term "security"

TABLE 4-1.   **Securities Exempted from Registration Under the Securities Act of 1933.**

1. U.S. government, including ones it guarantees
2. State or municipality, including ones it guarantees
3. Domestic banks or trust companies (but not bank holding
   companies)
4. Commercial paper or banker's acceptances maturing within nine
   months
5. Building and loan associations
6. Farmers' cooperative association
7. Common or contract carriers, such as railroads
8. Court-approved receivers' or trustees' certificates
9. Small business investment companies
10. Intrastate (see SEC Rule 147 in "Private Placement" section)
11. Religious, educational, charitable, or nonprofit
12. Insurance policies or mixed annuity contracts (but not variable
    annuities and variable life insurance policies)
13. Offerings that qualify under Regulation A of the Securities Act of
    1933. A less costly way to accomplish a distribution, Regulation A
    permits a qualified registration exemption for small yearly offerings
    of not over $1,500,000 by a corporation or for $100,000 by an
    affiliated person; however, it does require distribution of an
    informative offering circular.
14. Offerings that qualify under Regulation D of the Securities Act of
    1933. SEC Rules 501–506, under Regulation D, set forth the terms
    and conditions under which issuers can offer unregistered securities
    for sale in limited dollar amounts to a limited number of investors
    and/or to defined "accredited persons." For the most part these
    unregistered offerings are called private placements.

TABLE 4-2.   Transactions Exempted from Registration Under the Securities Act of 1933.

1. Those by anyone other than the issuer, a dealer, or an underwriter
2. Brokers' transactions that are not solicited from the customer (in other words, the customer takes the initiative)
3. Private placements (as opposed to public offerings)
4. Transactions by securities dealers (*except* when the dealers are still handling an unsold allotment of a registered new issue, or handling trades within 90 days of an initial public offering or 40 days of subsequent public offerings of that registered new issue)

calls to mind stocks and bonds, the Act defines a security as *any* note, stock, bond, evidence of debt, interest or participation in a profit-sharing agreement, investment contract, voting trust certificate, fractional undivided interest in oil, gas, or other mineral rights, or any warrant to subscribe to, or to purchase, any of the foregoing. Thus the 1933 Act, sometimes referred to as the "Full Disclosure Act," protects investors in any public offering by threatening those who willfully violate the law with fines of up to $10,000 and jail sentences of up to five years.

In addition to the registration statement, a **preliminary prospectus** must also be organized so that the group may have one available for prospective buyers to review. The preliminary prospectus, also called a **red herring** because of a red-lettered warning on the front page stating in effect that the document is not a final prospectus and should not be referred to as such, is a summary of pertinent details contained in the registration statement. It contains most of the facts known about the bond up to that moment. However, if it is used to solicit buy orders from investors, the investment banker is violating the Securities Act of 1933. While the registration statement is being reviewed by the SEC, the red herring is the only form of written communication allowed between the investment banker and the potential buyer. It is used primarily for gauging the degree of interest the investment banker's customers show for investing in that particular issue at that particular time. If it turns out that very few customers are interested in the issue, then the investment banker can cancel its membership in the syndicate group, before any commitments have been made and without facing any financial loss or penalty.

The Cooling-off Period

During the time that the SEC is reviewing the registration statement, several functions are being performed by the parties involved.

As mentioned earlier, the syndicate manager has formed the underwriting group and, during the cooling-off period, completes the formation of this group. Once the various investment bankers have agreed to underwrite the issue, other firms are approached by the syndicate manager to form the **selling group.** This group is not considered an official part of the syndicate, but primarily helps the syndicate to sell or distribute the bond issue at a fixed commission, and at the negotiated offering price.

As well as receiving approval by the Securities and Exchange Commission, the issue must also be approved for sale by all the states in which it will be distributed or sold. Unless the state government approves a bond issue for sale in that state, it cannot legally be offered for sale. This process is called **blue skying the issue.**

One of the more important activities taking place during the cooling-off period is the meeting of the officials of the corporation and the members of the underwriting group. At the **due diligence meeting,** all participating parties must attend because it is here that the prospectus is reviewed for accuracy and the terms of the underwriting are discussed. This is the last chance for members of the group to back out of the bond offer without facing penalties or being held liable for their part in the underwriting group.

A **final prospectus** is prepared during the due diligence meeting. This document is really just a condensation of the registration statement and preliminary prospectus. It is not officially "final" however, until the night before, or the morning of the day the issue can actually be sold, when the offer price and interest rate are determined to reflect fair terms based on the current overall market.

The length of the cooling-off period varies from issue to issue, but it generally lasts approximately 20 days. After the allotted time, the SEC either approves the bond issue for sale, delays it, or sometimes even aborts it. Assuming approval, the twentieth day then becomes the **effective date** or **public offering date:** the first day that the issue can be offered for sale to the public.

TRY THIS:

Corporate bonds and notes are brought to the public market through
a. Auctions.
b. An underwriting agreement.
c. Warrants.
d. Advertisement.

HERE'S WHY:

The correct answer is (b). The underwriting agreement is the contract between the investment banker and corporation, containing the final terms and prices of the issue. It is signed either on the evening before or early in the morning of the public offering date (effective date).

Agreement Among Underwriters

Soon after the due diligence meeting, the underwriters participating in the distribution draw up an agreement among themselves that specifies, among other things, the responsibilities of the manager, including the following:

Forming the Syndicate

Once part of a syndicate, an investment banker may safely assume that its association with the group will continue for all future underwritings in which any one of them acts as manager. In fact, once established as a significant distributor of securities in such offerings, an investment banker becomes recognized as a "major-bracket" participant, and its name is publicized near the top of the group's tombstone. (The tombstone will be explained later in this chapter.) The percentage of its underwriting commitment ranks equally with other major-bracket firms. Other investment bankers in those syndicates may be classified as submajor-, middle-major-, and minor-bracket underwriters, depending on their percentages of participation.

Once an underwriter has taken indications of interest and decides to participate in a group, it cannot buy a security in the marketplace for its own account or induce someone else to buy it while the distribution is pending.

Appointing a Selling Group

The manager also appoints other broker/dealers who agree to act as the underwriters' agents and to offer some of these securities to their customers. These firms make up what is known as the selling group. Each selling group member is allocated a portion of the issue to sell. Though selling group members follow the terms and restrictions of the underwriting agreement, they do not receive the full underwriters' spread, because they assume no individual responsibility or financial liability to the issuing corporation. Their **selling concession** may range from 25% to 75% of the spread, depending on how difficult it is to sell the issue.

The syndicate assumes the risk of making a profit on the underwriting. When the terms of the offering are finalized and the offering becomes effective, the underwriters (syndicate members) assume the liability of paying the corporation the net proceeds on settlement date—whether or not they are able to sell all or part of the issue. Moreover, only the reoffering price may be charged to customers, whether the customers buy from the syndicate or selling group members. Lower or higher sale prices are permitted only after the syndicate is terminated. While the selling group firms are not obliged to sell the issue—they may take as much or as little of the issue as they wish—the syndicate must make its profit during the offering and within the confines of the spread.

The compensation to the syndicate, selling group, and other dealers reflects the relative risk assumed by each type of participant. The greater compensation, represented by the spread, represents the greater risk, undertaken by the syndicate. The selling concession allowed selling group members is proportionate to their lesser risk.

Establishing the Underwriters' Retention ("the Pot")

The manager holds back a part of the issue (usually 25%) for allocation to the selling group and to institutional purchasers, who deal in large quantities. This reserved allocation is called "the pot." Since, in effect, each group member gets only 75% of its commitment, the manager's juggling of percentages is a touchy responsibility. Keeping everyone happy is hard to do.

Conducting Group Sales

Group sales are not sales made by the selling group. Rather, they are sales made out of the pot. If an institutional investor wants, say, $5,000,000 worth of bonds, the manager fills the order out of the pot rather than taking the securities from each of the underwriters. Unless the purchaser states otherwise, all syndicate members benefit pro rata according to their percentages of participation. Group sales are good stimulators. When the manager announces, "The pot is clean!" sellers find that orders come in more quickly because investors realize that institutions consider the offering a good investment.

Stabilizing the Market

Either on the effective date or within a couple of days thereafter, the underwriters begin making their public offering. At about the same time, the security begins trading openly in the marketplace. This trading activity is called the "aftermarket." Since the underwriters are bound to the terms of their agreement with the company, they cannot allow the market price to go much below the public offering price. So unless the offering is an immediate sellout, the managing underwriter is empowered to maintain a bid in the aftermarket at or perhaps slightly below the public offering price, on behalf of the syndicate. This syndicate bid may be continued for as long as necessary, but it usually only lasts several days.

This is the only time when manipulating a market price is legal. Ordinarily anyone found manipulating the market price of securities is subject to prosecution by the SEC under the terms of the Securities and Exchange Act of 1934. But stabilization to facilitate a bona fide distribution of securities is exempted from this restriction. Prompt notice, however, must be filed with the SEC and with the appropriate exchange.

When stabilizing aftermarket prices, the syndicate manager has no intention of repurchasing the entire issue. Often, the manager notifies participating firms that the stabilizing bid is made with a penalty attached. In this case, their customers should not enter the aftermarket to sell this new security at the price of the stabilizing bid. Otherwise, the member firms lose their spread or concession, are penalized so much per bond, or are not allowed to participate in future offerings.

A **penalty syndicate bid** is written into agreements between the underwriters and selling groups to ensure that participants strive to distribute the issue to investment portfolios and not to traders and speculators intent upon quick profits.

Although syndicate managers must make every attempt to maintain the public offering price, they have the authority to release members from that obligation if they see that the task has become hopeless. The security then fluctuates to its true level, as determined by market forces, even though the underwriters are still financially responsible to the issuer.

Allocating Hot Issues

Syndicate managers need not worry about maintaining the public offering price of "hot issues," which are securities that trade at an immediate premium in the aftermarket. This situation is a happy but delicate one. Using their business judgment, managers can legally oversell issues by up to 15% of the offering, because they will probably get that many cancellations.

Even if they do not, they can cover their short positions in one of two ways:

1. Managers can go into the aftermarket and buy the securities. This alternative is not considered a stabilization effort because the syndicate pays the offering price or more. Any loss sustained in this process, like the losses sustained in stabilization, is apportioned pro rata to each member.
2. The corporation can grant the underwriters an option or warrant to buy additional securities of the offering at a price below that of the public offering.

Sale of the Bond Issue

Now that the underwriting group has completed its main function (to organize the bond issue, set up the terms for sale, submit it for approval by the SEC), and the bond has been officially approved for sale, the syndicate members take center stage. They begin to contact their customers who earlier expressed an interest in the issue when the preliminary prospectus was circulated. Some of these customers may no longer be interested, some may be in different financial situations, and some may not have received the preliminary prospectus but may have heard about the issue through other sources or through their broker.

After the issue has been offered to the public and is actively and openly traded in the over-the-counter market, it is said to be in the aftermarket. If the new issue turns out to be very popular and the demand outweighs the supply, it is considered a **hot issue.** The price then rises to a premium (higher than the offering price), which offsets the supply-and-demand imbalance.

Advertising the Issue

To publicize the fact that a new offering has begun, the syndicate manager often takes out an advertisement in one or more newspapers or periodicals. The ad (Figure 4-2) is really just a notice with the important information listed. Any pizzazz or catchy phrases incorporated in the notice would render it illegal because, if it is mistakenly read as a solicitation, it must be accompanied by a prospectus. Because this ad appears so stolid and dull, the industry refers to it as a **tombstone.** Given its "homeliness," the tombstone can provide some very useful information. A sample is presented for you to follow in our discussion. Each important feature is given an identifying number and is described next.

FIGURE 4-2.   A Typical Tombstone.

① This announcement is neither an offer to sell nor a solicitation of an offer to buy any of these Securities.
The offer is made only by the Prospectus

② **$150,000,000**

BP North American Finance Corporation

9¼ % Guaranteed Debentures Due 2001

Payment of the principal of, premium, if any, and interest on the debentures is guaranteed by

The British Petroleum Company Limited

④ Interest payable February 1 and August 1

⑤ *Price 99½% and Accrued Income*

⑥ Copies of the Prospectus may be obtained in any State from only such of the
undersigned as may legally offer these Securities in compliance
with the securities laws of such State.

⑦ *MORGAN STANLEY & CO.*
Incorporated

GOLDMAN, SACHS & CO.

THE FIRST BOSTON CORPPORATION

MERRILL LYNCH, PIERCE, FENNER & SMITH
Incorporated

SALOMON BROTHERS

⑧

BACHE HALSEY STUART INC. BLYTH EASTMAN DILLION & CO.
Incorporated DILLION, READ & CO. INC.

DREXEL BURNHAM & CO. HORNBLOWER & WECKS-HEMPHILL, NOYES E.I HUTTON & COMPANY INC.

KIDDER, PEABODY & CO.
Incorporated KUHN, LOEB & CO. LAZARD FRERES & CO.

LEHMAN BROTHERS
Incorporated LOEB, RHOADES & CO. PAINE, WEBBER, JACKSON & CURTIS
Incorporated

REYNOLDS SECURITIES, INC. SMITH BARNEY, HARRIS-UPHAM & CO.
Incorporated WARBURG PARIBAS BECKER INC.

WERTHEIM & CO., INC. WHITE, WELD & CO.
Incorporated DEAN WITTER & CO.
Incorporated

BEAR, STEARNS & CO. L. F. ROTHSCHILD & CO. SHEARSON HAYDEN STONE INC.

SHIELDS MODEL ROLAND SECURITIES
Incorporated WEEDEN & CO.
Incorporated WOOD, STRUTHERS & WINTHROP, INC.

ABD SECURITIES CORPORATION BASLE SECURITIES CORPORATION ALEX, BROWN & SONS

EUROPARTNERS SECURITIES CORPORATION ROBERT FLEMING
Incorporated HILL SAMUEL SECURITIES
Incorporated

KLEINWORT, BENSON MOSELEY, HALLGARTEN & ESTABROOK INC.

NEW COURT SECURITIES CORPORATION OPPENHEIMER & CO., INC. R. W. PRESSPRICH & CO.
Incorporated

SOGEN-SWISS INTERNATIONAL CORP. THOMSON & McKINNON AUCHINCLOSS KOHLMEYER, INC.

SPENCER TRASK & CO.
Incorporated TUCKER, ANTHONY & R. L. DAY, INC. UBS-DB CORPORATION

AMERICAN SECURITIES CORPORATION ARNHOLD AND S. BLEICHROEDER, INC. J. C. BRADFORD & CO.

BUTCHER & SINGER

FAULKNER, DAWKINS & SULLIVAN, INC. LADENBURG, THALMANN & CO. INC.

MITCHELL HUTCHINS, INC. WM. E. POLLOCK & CO., INC.

THE ROBINSON-HUMPHREY COMPANY, INC. ELKINS, STROUD, SUPLEE & CO.

FAHNESTOCK & CO. GREENSHIELDS & CO. INC. JANNEY MONTGOMERY SCOTT INC.

KEEFE, BRUYETTE & WOODS, INC. NOMURA SECURITIES INTERNATIONAL, INC. STUART BROTHERS

C. E. UNTERBERG, TOWBIN CO. WILLIAM D. WITTER, INC. WOOD GUNDY INCORPORATED

1. This statement is required by the SEC and advises readers that the document is only an advertisement, not a solicitation.

2. This figure is the total par value of the bond, or the amount the corporation is hoping to obtain as a result of the loan. It is not the offering or current market value.

3. The name of the issuing company, interest rate, maturity date, and in this case the fact that the principal and interest payments are guaranteed by another larger corporation are all reflected in this portion of the ad.

4. Interest payments totaling 9.25% of par value ($92.50 per $1,000) will be paid each year until maturity. That is, $46.25 will be paid each February and August 1.

5. The offering price is fixed at 99.50% of par value ($995 per $1,000) plus interest accruable from February 13, 1989 to settlement date of the transaction.

6. This statement informs the reader that the issue may be offered by a particular underwriter only in those states in which that firm is registered to act as a broker/dealer and only according to the blue sky laws of that state.

7. The syndicate manager's name always appears at the top of the list of underwriters.

8. The principal underwriters of this issue appear in alphabetical but descending order according to their degree of financial responsibility for marketing the issue. Horizontal lines have been added to help distinguish the various groupings. The farther down the list, the less financial liability the firm has agreed to.

9. This is the effective date, the earliest date on which the public offering may begin.

TRY THIS:

An advertisement used for a public offering is called
a. A promo piece.
b. An announcement.
c. A fact sheet.
d. A tombstone.

HERE'S WHY:

The correct answer is (d). The tombstone very simply and durably lists all the facts about the new issue, taking care not to solicit readers to purchase. It is sometimes called the **offering circular**.

LET'S TRY ANOTHER ONE:

True or False? Corporate bonds are obligations issued by a state agency.

HERE'S WHY:

This statement is False. Corporate bonds are, obviously enough, issued by corporations. It is the firms' way of raising capital for a period of time, usually at a fixed rate.

Reading Bond Quotes

The average bond investor needs to know not only the name of the bond's issuer, but also the rate of interest the bond is paying and its maturity when undertaking a bond investment. This and other information can be obtained by reviewing the bond quotations in the financial section of the newspaper, or by calling a broker who has easy access to the quotation sheets published by the National Quotation Bureau. These quotation sheets indicate the prices on over-the-counter bonds which constitute the greatest number of bonds traded compared to the number traded on the New York Stock Exchange.

Figure 4-3 shows a portion from a corporate bond listing in the financial section of the newspaper. Let's look at the IBM $9\frac{3}{8}$ 04 in the left-hand column. The description "IBM $9\frac{3}{8}$ 04" means that the issuer of the bond is International Business Machines, that the bond has a $9\frac{3}{8}$% coupon (or nominal) rate, and that it matures in 2004. Bond investors and brokers would refer to this bond as "nine and

NEW YORK EXCHANGE BONDS

Tuesday, March 17

Total Volume $33,610,000

SALES SINCE JANUARY 1

1987	1986	1985
$2,085,513,000	$2,589,837,000	$1,841,393,000

	Domestic Tue.	Mon.	All Issues Tue.	Mon.
Issues traded	802	784	806	789
Advances	320	289	323	289
Declines	280	292	280	295
Unchanged	202	203	203	205
New highs	35	37	36	37
New lows	6	10	6	10

Dow Jones Bond Averages

—1985— High Low	—1986— High Low	—1987— High Low		———Tuesday——— —1987—	—1986—	—1985—
83.73 72.27	93.65 83.73	95.51 93.43	20 Bonds	94.77 +0.06	89.89 −0.02	72.32 −0.11
82.88 68.62	95.79 81.85	98.23 95.64	10 Utilities	97.08 +0.19	90.43 −0.07	68.97 −0.20
84.58 75.61	91.64 84.82	93.10 91.21	10 Industrial	92.46 −0.07	89.36 +0.03	75.68 −0.02

Bonds	Cur Yld	Vol	High	Low	Close	Net Chg.
Hutton 12s05	11.3	24	106⅜	106	106	− ⅝
IBM Cr 9⅞88	9.7	10	102	102	102	+ ⅜
IBM Cr 9⅜90	9.3	140	103¾	103¾	103¾	...
ICN 12⅞98	12.7	30	101⅝	101	101	− ¾
IdelB 9¼00f	...	25	92	89	92	+ 3
IllBel 8s04	8.3	15	96¾	96¾	96¾	− 1½
IllPw 10½04	10.0	10	105½	105½	105½	+ ½
IllPw 8⅝06	8.9	1	97	97	97	− 1
IllPw 9⅜16	9.2	25	102	102	102	...
Inco 12⅜10	12.0	20	103	103	103	...
IndBel 8⅛11	8.5	15	96	96	96	− ¾
IndBel 8⅛17	8.5	10	95⅛	95⅛	95⅛	− 1⅜
Inexc 8½00	cv	32	91	90⅝	90⅝	...
InldStl 9½00	10.1	5	93⅞	93⅞	93⅞	+ 1¾
InldStl 7.9s07	10.3	36	76½	76½	76½	...
InldStl 11¼90	11.2	292	100¾	99⅝	100½	− ¼
ItgRs 10¾96	10.8	33	99½	99¼	99½	+ ¼
Intlgc 11.99s96	12.8	15	94	93⅞	94	+ ½
Intrfst 7¾05	cv	30	69	68½	69	...
IBM 9⅜04	8.9	111	105⅛	105	105	...
IBM 7⅞04	cv	414	122¼	121	122	+ ¾
IBM 10¼95	9.1	8	113	113	113	− 1
IPap 8.85s95	8.7	10	102	102	102	...
IntRec 9s10	cv	8	86	85	86	...
Intnr 10½08	cv	90	135	131½	135	+ 3¾
Intnr 11s95	10.2	10	108	108	108	+ 2¼
Ipco 5¼89	5.6	4	94½	94½	94½	

Bonds	Cur Yld	Vol	High	Low	Close	Net Chg.
Mobil 13.76s04	12.0	27	115⅛	115⅛	115⅛	...
Monog 10s99	11.0	10	91	91	91	...
Mons 8⅜408	8.7	75	100¾	100¾	100¾	− ¼
MonW 4⅞90	5.2	57	93	92½	93	...
MonW 9⅜00	9.3	4	100½	100½	100½	+ ⅛
MntWC 6½287	6.5	2	99½	99½	99½	...
MntWC 9¼90	9.2	5	101	101	101	− ½
MntWC 9.6s95	9.1	15	105⅜	105⅜	105⅜	...
Morgn 4¾98	cv	10	234	234	234	...
MtSTI 9¾12	9.2	34	106	105½	106	+ ½
MtSTI 9⅝15	9.1	9	105¼	105¼	105¼	...
MtSTI 8⅝18	8.7	10	99¼	99¼	99¼	+ ¼
NBD 8¼10	cv	40	134	134	134	...
NBI 8¼07	cv	1	77	77	77	+ ½
NLInd 7½95	9.0	145	83	82	83	+ 2
NWA 7½10	cv	31	126	126	126	− 1
NConv 9s08	cv	15	90¾	90¾	90¾	− ¼
NtEdu 6½211	cv	30	115½	115	115	...
NEnt 4¾96	cv	3	58	58	58	+ 1
NtGyp zr04	...	757	61½	60	61½	+ 1
NMed 9s06	cv	113	114¾	114½	114⅜	+ ⅛
NMed 8s08	cv	187	103⅞	103½	103½	− ⅜
NMed 12¾499A	11.8	5	107⅞	107⅞	107⅞	+ 2⅝
NMed 12⅛99B	11.5	5	105⅛	105	105	− ⅛
NMEd 12s00	11.4	10	105	105	105	...
NMed 12½00	11.8	25	106½	106	106	− ½
NMed zr04	...	252	22¾		22¾	¾

FIGURE 4-3. Reading the Bond Quotations.

three-eighths of oh-four." This information tells you two things: first, that the bond will pay $93.25 in interest each year, in two semiannual payments of $46.625 each, and, second, that it will pay the holder of the face value of $1,000.

Skip the next column, labeled "Cur Yld" for now.

The column headed "Vol" tells you the number of IBM bonds traded that day. In this case, 111 bonds were traded.

The "High," "Low," and "Close" columns provide a record of price fluctuations during the trading day. The highest price at which IBM traded for the day was $105\frac{1}{8}$, and the lowest was 105—the same price at which it closed.

Remember that bond quotations are not read the same as stock quotations. In stock trading, "$95\frac{1}{8}$" means "$95.125." In bond trading, "$95\frac{1}{8}$" means "$951.25." In other words, a "point" in a stock price is $1, but a "point" in bond trading is $10. More about points in Chapter 8.

The "Net Chg." (net change) column marks the change in the closing price from the last day's closing price. The IBM $9\frac{3}{8}$ 04 did not change in price from the day before. The IBM $7\frac{7}{8}$ 04, on the next line down, went up $\frac{3}{4}$ point ($7.50), as indicated by the plus sign. So yesterday's closing was $121\frac{1}{4}$ ($122 - \frac{3}{4}$). The IBM bond below the $7\frac{7}{8}$ 04 went down a full point ($10), so that yesterday's close was 114 (113 + 1).

Now let's go back to the "Cur Yld" (current yield) column. Because the price of the IBM $9\frac{3}{8}$ 04 bond (105, or $1,050) is higher than the face value ($1,000), it is said to be trading at a premium. Because the buyer has to pay more to own the bond, the yield on the investment is reduced. So if you apply the current yield formula to this bond, you will find that the current yield for IBM $9\frac{3}{8}$ 04 bond is 8.9%—just the figure shown in the column.

A bond that is selling for less than the face amount, such as the IntRec 9s10 a little farther down the column, is said to be trading at a discount. Because the discount in the price represents less of an investment outlay for the buyer, the percentage return is higher than if the bond were trading at par, that is, at its face value.

The bond quotation tables in the newspapers usually have an index of terms and abbreviations to help you decipher the listing. The only thing it does not spell out for you is the full name of the bond issuer. A broker can probably help you out with any questions you may have.

Corporate Bond Issuers

Corporate bonds are usually classified by type of issuer in the following way:

Industrial.

Utility.

Transportation.

Financial and banking.

Industrial Bonds

The industrial bond group is the most generic and largest of the four groups because it includes the widest variety of corporations. Merchandising, manufacturing, service, retailing, and wholesaling companies fall into this category. They are issued to finance physical corporate expansion in the form of additional buildings, to increase working capital, or to refund a previous bond issue.

Utility Bonds

Companies that provide electric power, telephone service, gas distribution, and water and sewage capabilities to the public issue utility bonds.

Transportation Bonds

Companies dealing with forms of transportation such as airlines, railroad companies, trucking firms, and even cargo ships issue the transportation bond. The **railroad equipment trust** and **equipment trust certificates** fall into this category.

Financial and Banking Bonds

Issuers of finance bonds include banks, finance and loan companies, insurance companies, and real estate investment companies. These companies borrow money at a certain interest rate so that they can lend that money to other firms or investors at a higher interest rate. The difference between the rates becomes their profit. Money serves as their main asset and collateral instead of equipment or real estate.

Other Issuers

International bonds are characterized by principal and interest payments according to the currency denomination of the country where they are issued. Investors can choose to invest in bond issues available in British pounds sterling, German marks, Dutch guilders, or Swiss francs.

Types of Corporate Bonds

Mortgage Bonds

The most common and oldest form of secured obligation or collateral used by corporations is the **mortgage bond.** Companies that invest heavily in their equipment and buildings usually issue these types of bonds. In this case, the investor is protected by the real assets of the firm, such as the equipment and real estate. The property is generally worth more than the money borrowed, so if the company defaults, the investors can claim the property to satisfy the loan.

Debentures

A **debenture** is an unsecured bond. That is, the firm does not have any real assets to "back up" the bond; there is no collateral except for the reputation and good name of the borrowing firm. The firm's general assets and earnings determine the bond's security.

Collateral Trust Bonds

The **collateral trust bond** is backed by other securities or the collateral of another corporation. Most likely, the issuing company owns stock in another company or perhaps a subsidiary company. The strength of the other company is what supports the bond issue.

Guaranteed Bonds

As a flip side to the collateral trust bond, investors can consider the **guaranteed bond.** These bonds use the assets and/or creditworthiness of another corporation to back the bond they have issued. In many cases, a parent company, for instance, guarantees the payment of interest and principal of the bond issued by a subsidiary company.

Equipment Trust Bonds

Instead of pledging real estate, creditworthiness, or reputation, **equipment trust bonds** are backed by machinery, such as trains, planes, and trucks. The bondholder is protected by the value of the equipment.

TRY THIS:

Which type of bond is unsecured?
a. Mortgage.
b. Collateral trust.
c. Equipment trust.
d. Debenture.

HERE'S WHY:

The correct answer is (d). The debenture does not offer any "real" assets to back up the bond. The only collateral going for it is the company's good name and reputation.

Convertible Bonds

A **convertible bond** gives the bondholder the option to convert bonds to a particular number of shares of common stock at a specified price per share. This enables the owner to have a fixed income source during the life of the bond, and later, if the value of the common shares of the company's stock increases, the owner can convert ownership from bonds to stock.

TRY THIS:

A corporate security considered most secure from the viewpoint of underlying collateral is the
a. Equipment trust certificate.
b. Prior lien bond.
c. Subordinated debenture.
d. Voting trust certificate.

HERE'S WHY:

The correct answer is (a). Equipment trust bonds pledge machinery, such as trains, trucks, and planes, as collateral for loans used to buy the machinery. Because all companies within a given industry use basically the same machinery, if a company defaults, it can sell the equipment easily, and thus bondholders are protected.

Income Bonds

Income bonds are long term and issued with a high interest rate. It is also an unusual type of bond because the issuing company is usually in or near bankruptcy and only pays interest if it earns enough money (by a specified date) to make such a payment. If earnings are there, but insufficient to make the required interest payments, then payment is usually made in proportion to the earnings. The principal, however, is always paid upon maturity of the bond.

Floating Rate Bonds

Floating rate bonds periodically increase or decrease their interest rate to coincide with the interest rates in the bond market in general. They offer investors a fixed income investment with a built-in hedge against inflation and rising interest rates.

TRY THIS:

A client who wishes to have his debt security backed by a lien on property will choose any of the following except
a. A debenture.
b. A mortgage bond.
c. Equipment trust bond.
d. A collateral trust bond.

HERE'S WHY:

The correct answer is (a). This is the only issue that does not offer any real asset or property as collateral protection for creditors.

Zero-Coupon Bonds

The **zero-coupon bond** has exactly what its name implies—no coupon. It does not offer any interest payments over the life of the bond, only payment of the full face value upon maturity. It does provide a deep discount of the face value to the interested investor. The "interest," then, is the difference between the discount price and the face value.

Commodity-Backed Bonds

The face value of **commodity-backed bonds** is usually linked to commodity prices that are forecast to stay on top of inflation. For example, a corporation may want to issue a bond that is indexed to the price of silver, providing that the price of that commodity is expected to rise and stay above the overall inflation rate.

Junk Bonds

In passing, you have probably seen or heard the term **junk bonds.** This concept is new to the area of corporate bonds and debt financing.

Junk bonds get their name because of the low rating they carry (in most instances, **B** or below). The assets securing the debt are highly leveraged and/or the proceeds are being raised for the specific purpose of financing a merger or acquisition.

The rating services view junk bonds as lacking a fundamental economic purpose. However, both individuals and institutions have made substantial profits from junk bonds. For example, at one point junk bonds offered a yield of 14% or better. As interest rates declined, the prices of the bonds appreciated to adjust to the new prevailing rates of 10% or below.

Refunding Bonds

This type of bond is used to pay off an older, previously issued bond, usually to save interest. If a bond was issued at a particularly high interest rate, the corporation may wish to pay off the debt and refinance the loan at a more favorable, lower interest rate to save money in interest payments.

Money Market Instruments

This type of short-term debt security has a maturity of less than one year, is usually issued at a discount, and does not pay any interest. Details of these instruments are discussed in Chapter 7.

TRY THIS:

A corporation has outstanding $75 million of a 7¾% convertible debenture due June 1, 1991. Management decides to replace that obligation with $125 million of a 9% straight-debt security maturing in 2005. If a portion of the proceeds from the new issue is used to retire the convertible bonds, we can say that the debt was extinguished through

a. Refunding.
b. Forced conversion.
c. A sinking fund.
d. Open market purchases.

HERE'S WHY:

The correct answer is (a). If a company decides to combine several out-standing loans under a single new indenture, it can simultaneously call the old bonds and publicly offer for sale the new debt security. The new bond is then called a consolidated, general, or refunding mortgage bond.

5
Municipal Securities

Municipal Debt

Debt securities issued by states, cities, townships, counties, and other political subdivisions are known as municipal bonds or securities. The money that is raised by these bonds is used to build roads, bridges, industrial parks, schools, and many other projects. Municipal bonds, or "munis," as they are often affectionately called, provide the finances necessary to fuel growth and generate new income for the local government.

Prior to the Tax Reform Act of 1986 (TRA), all municipal bonds were exempt from federal income taxes, and some were exempt from state and local taxes if held by residents of the issuing municipality. With the passing of the TRA, not all municipals are tax-exempt.

The 1986 Act distinguishes between municipal bonds issued before August 15, 1986 and those issued after that date (with exceptions, of course). Any munis issued prior to this date retain any of the tax-exempt features that they offered before it. Any municipal issued after this date falls into one of three categories, depending on its purpose.

1. **Public purpose bonds**, issued directly by the state or local authority, are used for the traditional "municipal" projects, such

as a new school building or highway improvement program (programs that are clearly the responsibility of government). These munis are tax-exempt.

2. **Private activity bonds**, although issued by the state or local government, supply funds for "private" projects, like a sports arena, shopping mall, or civic center. These bonds are subject to federal taxation, but they may be exempt from state/local taxation in the states in which they are issued.

3. **Nongovernmental purpose bonds** raise funds for "nongovernmental" (but not "private") uses, such as housing or student loans. These are tax-exempt, but (a) the TRA puts a cap on the amount that a municipality may issue of such bonds, and (b) the interest is treated as a preference item for purposes of the alternative minimum tax.

As a result, the phrase "municipal bonds" may no longer be considered synonomous with the term "tax-exempts." Although a tax-exempt municipal bond's interest payments (usually on a semiannual basis) are exempted from federal taxation, any profit from its purchase or sale is *not* exempt. In some instances, the interest payments are also free of state and local taxation, usually on the condition that the bondholder lives in the same state as the issuer. This triple exemption is always a feature of some issues, such as those of Puerto Rico, the Virgin Islands, the Trust Territory, and Washington, D.C. Because these payments are tax-free, municipal issues generally carry lower interest rates than do corporate or U.S. government bonds.

Underwriting the Municipal Bond

Municipal bonds are brought to market through two methods. **Negotiated offerings**, similar to most corporate underwritings, are normally seen in revenue bond offerings. Municipals have no filing requirement or cooling-off period, as corporate bonds do. Each buyer receives a copy of the official statement instead of a prospectus. The official statement provides the buyer with information similar to what is found in a prospectus. When a bond is negotiated, an investment banking firm, or group of firms, reaches an agreement directly with an issuer concerning interest to be paid on the bond, maturities, and so on. The issuer sells the issue to the group of investment bankers offering them at the lowest net cost, and the investment bankers reoffer those bonds to the investing public.

Most general obligation bonds are offered via **competitive bid**. (See Figure 5-1.) The municipal bond issuer publishes an official notice of sale notifying underwriters who previously bid for offerings by that issuer. The official notice of sale gives specific details of the prospective offering such as type, size, date for the bids to be delivered, paying agent, purpose of the issue, and maturity dates. It also invites interested parties to submit bids for the offering. After examination by the municipality, an underwriting group who has the bid for the lowest net interest cost to the municipality is awarded the bond. In short, investment banking firms or groups of such firms must submit bids to the issuer of a bond offering for the purchase of the entire issue.

In addition to determining the type of bond to be offered, the financial adviser for the issuer of the bond also helps to set up a repayment schedule. Issuers have three options: serial bonds, term bonds, or a split offering.

Usually, general obligation bonds are issued in serial form; that is, they mature in stages. The issuer's purpose is often to maintain level debt service.

When a serial municipal bond issue comes to market, the managing underwriter writes a **scale** that lists

1. the dollar amount maturing in each year.
2. the appropriate offering price (stated as a percentage of par or as a basis price, as the case may be).

If the yields are lower in the shorter-term than in the longer-term maturities, it is known as a **normal scale**. If the shorter-term yields are higher than longer-term yields, the scale is said to be **inverted**.

Generally used for revenue offerings, all term bonds mature on a single date, and they are frequently paid out of a sinking fund. Term bonds may be quoted in dollar amounts and in this case are referred to as **dollar bonds**.

A split offering combines serial and term bonds in a single offering.

Regardless of type, municipal bonds are almost always callable prior to maturity, often with a 10-year call protection and a sinking fund schedule. If bonds are called, they will be called by inverse order

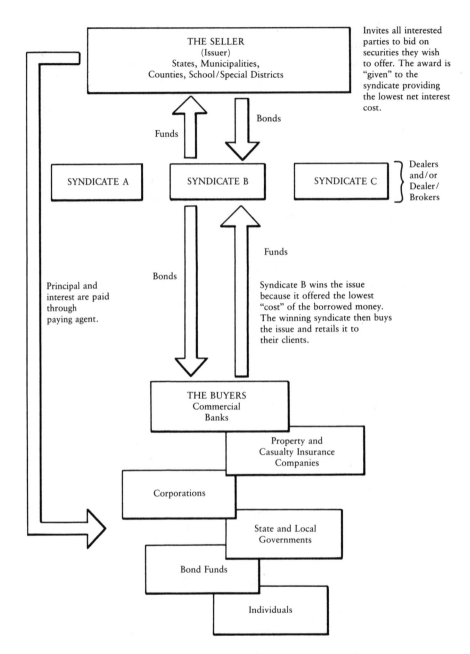

FIGURE 5-1.   The Competitive Bidding Process.

of maturity; that is, the longest maturity will be called first. Within a given maturity, the bond numbers selected for redemption are chosen by a lottery.

TRY THIS:

Which of the following most closely resembles a prospectus for a registered negotiated offering?
a. An official notice of sale.
b. A sealed bid.
c. An invitation to tender.
d. An official statement.

HERE'S WHY:

The correct answer is (d). Since most municipal bonds are exempt securities, there is no 1933 Act registration filing requirement and consequently no prospectus. However, most states make what is in effect "full disclosure" by distributing to purchasers of a new issue a prospectuslike brochure called an **official statement**.

TRY THIS:

Municipal term bonds are typically quoted
a. On a discount basis.
b. On a current yield basis.
c. On a nominal yield basis.
d. In dollars.

HERE'S WHY:

The correct answer is (d). Term bonds are sometimes priced on a YTM basis but are also seen frequently quoted in dollar prices. Thus the name dollar bonds is sometimes applied to them.

The Underwriter

The underwriter of a municipal bond may not be one individual investment firm. Because municipalities often sell large blocks of bonds in amounts of over $25 million and up to $500 million, it is unrealistic for one firm to handle the entire issue. Financial limitations and risk factors warrant the involvement of any number of investment banking firms for the successful sale of the bonds.

For an underwriter to be successful, its trading and sales departments must be alert in determining the proper marketplace for the bond and quickly assess the best way to reach prospective buyers. Decisions regarding procedures, rules, and technicalities involved in underwriting an issue must often be made on the spur of the moment. Many of these firms are bidding for 10 or 12 issues a day and actually underwriting up to 10 issues a week, so speed and agility with snap decisions is crucial.

The Syndicate

As mentioned earlier, depending on the size of the issue being offered, underwriters may join together in a syndicate to spread the risk of the sale and to gain wider access to prospective investors. This temporary association of broker/dealers is directed by a senior manager, and jointly, they sell the new bond issue to the public. Normally the syndicate has a lifetime of 30 days, although it can be disbanded if it sells the bonds sooner.

Syndicates fall into two general categories:

1. Eastern (undivided) account.
2. Western (divided) account.

The **Eastern (undivided) account** is the more popular type of syndicate. Each member is responsible for selling at least an agreed percentage of the issue. If a member, however, cannot distribute its participation, the other members become responsible for a percentage of that unsold portion. The account is "undivided" regarding selling as liability because as an Eastern account, it forces the members to join together in completing the distribution.

TRY THIS:

In an Eastern syndicate offering $25,000,000 in bonds, a member has a 10% participation. If that member has already sold $2,500,000 in bonds, the member's liability for further sales is
a. 0.
b. 10% of any remaining unsold portion.
c. $250,000.
d. $2,500,000.

HERE'S WHY:

The correct answer is (b). An Eastern syndicate is united as to both underwriting and selling liabilities. Therefore, even though a member may have sold his indicated $2,500,000 (10% of the total $25,000,000 offering), that member is still liable for any unsold portion in the same proportion. If the syndicate had $1,000,000 in unsold bonds, such a member would have the liability for $100,000 beyond the original participation.

The **Western (divided) account** is the less common type of syndicate in which each member is responsible only for its own participation, with no liability for other members' unsold bonds. This type of account is sometimes seen in an offering of municipal term bonds. This is where all bonds in the issue carry the same coupon rate and maturation date.

Once the issuer designates the syndicate, both parties sign an underwriting agreement. The senior manager then issues a release letter, sometimes called a **syndicate account letter**, to the syndicate members. The letter describes the purchase of the bonds, names the account manager who will keep the records, and describes the *priority of orders*. This describes which types of orders will be filled first. The priority is usually as follows:

Presale orders—orders received by the syndicate before the actual award of the issue.

Group account orders—orders that are credited to the whole account. These orders are credited according to each member's
participation in the offering.

Designated orders—orders from customers who specify which
syndicate member is to fill it.

Member takedown orders—the last orders to be filled. In these,
the member will take the bonds from the account at the takedown price (the price the syndicate member pays when bonds
are taken from the account). The member will get the whole
spread.

In either the Eastern or Western type of underwriting, the essential business structure is the same: the syndicate buys the bonds from
the issuer at one price and resells them at a slightly higher price for
a profit. The firms charge no commissions on the sales of the bonds
because they are acting as "dealers" or as "principals." Either term
means that they buy and sell for their own accounts. They may charge
a commission only when they execute trades in behalf of clients, that
is, when they act as "brokers" or as "agents."

Who's Who in Municipal Underwriting

The municipal department of the dealer is usually made up of the
following:

1. The **underwriting** or **syndicate, area** consists of one or more
   people who decide on and conduct underwritings. They set
   prices and yields on new issues, sit in on price meetings, co-
   ordinate with other dealers, and keep the firm's traders and
   sales staff up-to-date on upcoming offerings.
2. The **traders** do not actively participate in selling a new issue.
   Instead, they buy and sell the bonds in the "secondary" market, after the primary offering is complete. Nevertheless, they
   need to be informed of pending issues to prepare for maintaining an inventory of the bonds later on. Larger trading sections have traders who specialize in types of municipal bonds.
3. The **sales staff** become very involved in primary offerings.
   While the syndicate personnel may evaluate the salability of

a new issue and price it approximately, the salespeople are the ones who actually make the calls and make the sales.

In an underwriting, the syndicate, sales, and trading people all sit in a large room that is equipped for trading. Before them are quotation consoles and phone systems that link them with customers and other members of the dealer community. The offering itself, if priced properly and sold aggressively, is often sold out within the day.

4. The **public finance group** has the task of drumming up new negotiated underwritings and may offer their services as financial advisory for a fee.

   Commercial banks, forbidden by law to become involved in general obligation (GO) bond offerings (which are usually offered in negotiated underwritings), have a financial advisory group, not a public finance group. They can still, however, have a "new business" staff, whose aim is to generate new housing and education revenue bonds.

5. **Municipal research** has assumed greater importance in the 1980s, when it became apparent that municipal issuers could default (New York City in 1975 being the finest example). While at one time the rating agencies were the sole source of credit information on state and local issues, municipal research sections have come to be increasingly vital to successful underwritings. Generally, this department prepares a concise opinion before the dealer makes a commitment in a negotiated offering or a bid in a competitive deal.

6. **Operations** processes orders, issues payment checks, takes and makes deliveries of securities, and performs other required recordkeeping functions. This area, also known as the **back office**, is responsible for "clearing" the trades that the firm makes either with or on behalf of its customers and other dealers.

The Spread and Pricing

Spread and Takedown

As part of the underwriting procedure, the syndicate buys the bonds from the issuer at a discount from the public offering price. The difference, called the **spread**, is the maximum gross profit in the municipal underwriting. The manager allocates the bonds to the syndicate members at the offering price less the **takedown**. The takedown is usually 1 to 2 points ($10 to $20 per $1,000 principal amount). The bonds are then sold to the public.

EXAMPLE:

The syndicate buys each bond in an offering at a $1\frac{1}{2}$-point discount. For each $1,000 bond, it pays $985 to the issuer. The spread, therefore, is $1\frac{1}{2}$ points, or $15. If the takedown is $1\frac{1}{4}$ points, each syndicate member buys its bonds at $987.50 each ($1,000.00 − $12.50) and then offers them to the public at par. The managing underwriter keeps a $\frac{1}{4}$ point per bond, and each member keeps $1\frac{1}{4}$ points.

Selling Concession

Occasionally a nonmember of the syndicate has a client order to fill and buys from syndicate members to fill it. The nonmember's compensation is the **selling concession**. It is included in the takedown.

EXAMPLE:

If the takedown is 1 point and the selling concession is $\frac{5}{8}$ of a point, the nonmember makes $6.25 ($\frac{5}{8}$) on the sale, and the member makes the other $3.75 ($\frac{3}{8}$). This is typical—it reflects the fact that selling is usually more difficult than risk taking.

The Competitive Underwriting

Whereas in a negotiated offering the issuer approaches the underwriter directly, a competitive underwriting involves many more steps, the first of which is for the issuer to make its intentions known to prospective underwriters.

By law, competitive bidding must be used for the underwriting of general obligation bonds. To solicit bids, the issuer publishes an **official notice of sale** in the financial news and in legal publications.

Active issuers also generally send copies of the notice to dealers they have worked with in the past.

An ad in the municipal bond's trade paper, *The Daily Bond Buyer,* is a must. Anyone who is involved in munis reads this paper—especially those in the syndicate departments of dealer firms. This paper itemizes most negotiated and competitive issues in one of three sections: "proposed new issues," "invitations for bids," and "official municipal bond notices." It also offers a yield worksheet service, "new issue worksheet and record service," that has become accepted industrywide.

Another source of bond information is *The Blue List.* Bonds available for resale in the secondary market are listed by state, along with such information as the number of bonds offered, issuer, maturity date, coupon rate, price, and dealer making the offering. Ratings are not included, but there are sections on settlement dates of recent new offerings, prerefunded bonds, and miscellaneous offerings (some U.S. government and agency obligations, railroad equipment trust certificates, corporate bonds, and even preferred stocks). The dollar value of listings, referred to as the **floating supply,** gives an indication of the size and liquidity of the secondary municipal market.

TRY THIS:

Which of the following can be found in *The Blue List?*
  I. Bond prices.
 II. Bond yields.
III. Bond ratings.
IV. Bond maturity dates.

a. I only.
b. III and IV only.
c. I, II, and IV only.
d. I, II, III, and IV.

HERE'S WHY:

The correct answer is (c). *The Blue List* is published daily by a division of Standard & Poor's. It contains secondary market offerings of municipal bonds, identified by

1. Amount offered.
2. Issue.
3. Coupon.
4. Maturity.
5. YTM/price.
6. Firm making the offering.
Ratings are not mentioned. Also included are some listings of corporate bond and preferred stock offerings.

As a firm bids on upcoming bond issues, the syndicate people keep the salespeople current, usually in a Monday morning meeting. At these meetings, each issue is received and a sales strategy is devised.

The actual competitive bidding process on a particular issue begins with an opinion from the research staff. While municipal issuers call on rating agencies to rate their offerings, the syndicate staff in the brokerage firm generally wants an independent evaluation. The second opinion, if strong enough, may prompt the firm to put in an aggressive bid, on the assumption that, given an assurance of selling out the issue, it can offer a lower net interest cost to the issuer. Of course, if the research department's analysis is weak, the dealer may not even submit a bid.

Price Meetings

To come up with a competitive bid, syndicate members hold several "price meetings." Preliminary price meetings, held one or two days before the bid must be submitted, are low-keyed. Representing each syndicate member, one or more members of the syndicate groups discuss the salability of the impending offering and other similar issues such as spread, prices, and yields. One of the main topics is the "reoffering scale," which is the array of prices and yields for each maturity in the issue. These prices and yields are entered onto *The Bond Buyer* worksheets.

The overall goal is to reach agreement on a set of yields for the new bonds that balances two objectives: (2) To keep yields high enough to attract investors and to make the issue salable and (2) to be low enough to win the bid. To issuers, interest represents cost, so the lower the interest, the better. That is why competitive bids are awarded on the basis of net interest cost, that is, whichever syndicate offers to buy the issue at the lowest yield.

At the end of the preliminary meeting, the syndicate turns its proposed scale over to the salespeople, who proceed to solicit orders from the firm's clients. The number of orders taken at this time is a reliable indicator of whether the issue can be sold out at the proposed scale.

About an hour before the bid is due, the manager holds the final price meeting, which is usually more tense than the first meeting. The meeting begins with the manager presenting the proposed scale, maybe suggesting the spread, and reporting on orders and on the latest developments in the muni bond market. Then, members suggest other scales, sometimes disagree, and even occasionally drop out of the syndicate. While orders continue to come in (with some issues selling out before the meeting is over), members argue for a wider spread or lower scale. The last order of business is the order period—the time during which orders are taken (usually one or two hours).

Only minutes before the deadline, the final scale is calculated and the bid is phoned to the person who is to deliver it to the issuing municipality. The manager is responsible for ensuring that the sealed bid is delivered, usually by hand, to the municipality. With the bid goes a good-faith check for about 2% of the total value of the issue, which the municipality may use if the dealer fails to deliver the proceeds of the sale.

With all the bids in hand, the municipality computes the net interest cost of each and awards the issue to the dealer with the lowest one.

If their syndicate is the winner, the salespeople start selling immediately. From this point on, competitive and negotiated underwritings are the same. In both types of offerings, the senior manager has, by the time selling begins, issued a release letter or agreement among underwriters to the syndicate members.

During the selling period, the manager performs a number of other duties, including

1. Keeping the books for the syndicate.
2. Confirming orders over the phone when the order period is over.

Dating

Municipal bonds are arbitrarily "dated" as of the first or fifteenth of the month of issuance. The **offering date**, decided by the underwriters, is the date on which the bonds are sold to the public. Due to possible delays for printing the bonds and other legal procedures, the bonds are offered on a **when**, **as**, and **if issued** basis. That is, the firm will sell and deliver the bonds *when* they are issued, *as* they are issued, and *if* they are issued. Normally, the bonds are delivered about three to four weeks after the offering date. Interest accrues to the seller from the **dated date**, and it continues to accrue up to but not including the settlement date.

To Sell or Not to Sell

Issues that are in great demand (hot issues) can sell out in a couple of hours. Usually, however, bonds are left after the order period, and orders are taken on a first-come, first-served basis. The syndicate is disbanded when the issue is sold out. Most syndicates run for 30 days, but the members can renew if need be. Few offerings run that long, though. When an issue does not sell in 30 days, the syndicate can change the terms of the offering, which usually requires the majority consent of the members.

If the issue still cannot be sold, the issue can be distributed among the members or given to a "bond broker."

A bond broker (or broker's broker) trades only with other dealers. These firms do not deal directly with investors. Of approximately 20 or so such dealers in the country, most are located in New York City. Municipal bond dealers turn to these brokers when they want to sell bonds out of their inventories or buy bonds for inventory. When selling, bond brokers gather bids from other brokers; this is called the "bid-wanted" business. When buying, they circulate the fact that they are willing to buy a particular bond at a stated yield or price.

When an issue proves to be particularly difficult to sell, the remaining bonds can be given to one broker or to a group of them. The brokers then put the bonds out for the bid, and syndicate members can, like any other dealer, bid for the bonds. The one with the best bid gets the bonds.

TRY THIS:

The "dated date" on a new municipal bond offering refers to
a. The date of the official notice of sale.
b. The date when the bonds are available for delivery.
c. The settlement date.
d. The date from which interest begins to accrue.

HERE'S WHY:

The correct answer is (d). Every tombstone on a new municipal offering has an item such as "dated February 1." This means that a purchaser of the new issue will pay the principal amount plus accrued interest from the dated date. Because of the necessary delays in printing certificates and obtaining the final legal opinion, there may be a considerable delay between the dated date and the settlement date.

After the Offering

After the sale of the issue, while certificates are printed, the manager has to wrap things up. The first order of business is a letter to syndicate members stating the **reoffering terms**, that is, the terms by which the bonds are to be offered to investors and other buyers. Such terms include the spread, takedown, and concession. The letter also explains how the issue will be advertised and how members will be represented in the ad. (Syndicate members are generally listed in accordance with the degree of their participation, with the greater contributors at the top of the ad.)

When the bonds are ready for delivery, all payments are made. To pay the issuer, the manager arranges a loan from a commercial bank. If the manager or any other member of the syndicate is a bank, it may extend the loan. The check to the issuer is for the amount agreed upon less the good-faith deposit. The bonds are then delivered and distributed to the members, who fill orders and channel payments for the orders back to the manager. With all payments in hand, the manager retires the loan, distributes the profits among members, and issues a final statement of participations, expenses, and profits. And to think, all this takes only a few days.

TRY THIS:

The winning syndicate in a competitive offering is the one that
a. Bids for the largest number of bonds.
b. Bids for the highest coupon.
c. Bids for the highest net interest cost.
d. Bids for the lowest net interest cost.

HERE'S WHY:

The correct answer is (d). The municipality naturally wants to sell to the "high bidder," but this does not mean the most dollars, since all syndicates are competing to buy an entire issue of a fixed amount. The winning syndicate will be that which is able to achieve the lowest overall costs (net interest cost) to the municipality.

Types of Municipal Bonds

Municipal bonds can be divided into several different types (see Table 5-1).

General obligation bonds (GOs) are issued by states, cities, towns, or counties. All GO bonds are, in one way or another, backed by the taxing power of the issuer. They are referred to as **full faith and credit bonds**. Defaults are rare, and principal and interest are paid regularly.

When a legal limit is imposed on the taxing power of the issuer, general obligation bonds are then called **limited tax bonds**. Taxes may not be raised indefinitely to cover the debt. Bonds that are not restricted in this way are called **unlimited tax bonds.**

Generally, states have greater taxing powers than their political (local) subdivisions—cities, town, counties—and they usually rely on personal and corporate income taxes, as well as on sales, gasoline, or highway use taxes, as security. Since local issuers don't have the taxing powers of states, they usually rely on **ad valorem** (assessed valuation) **taxes** to back their GOs. Such taxes, the most common source of security revenue, are often levied in mills per dollar of assessed valuation (a mill equals one-tenth of one cent).

Special assessment bonds are secured by an assessment on those who benefit directly from the project, be it street lights or sidewalks.

TABLE 5-1.   **Summary of Municipal Bonds**

Type	Issuers	Backing	Types/Remarks
General obligation (GO)	States, cities, towns, counties.	"Full faith and credit" of issuer (i.e., personal and corporate income taxes, sales, gasoline, and highway-use taxes).	*Limited*—legal limit on debt-related taxation; *unlimited*—no such legal limit.
Limited tax bonds	"	Ad valorem taxes.	
Special assessment	"	Assessments on those who benefit by facility.	
Revenue	Agency, district, or authority—the issuer is created by legislation.	Fees, taxes, tolls, or other revenues from facility constructed by raised funds.	*Double-barreled*— backed also by taxing power ("full faith and credit") of underlying municipality or state.
Industrial development	"	Revenues from net lease between issuing agency and industrial corporation.	Issuing authority constructs facility and long-term leases it to industrial corporation.
Special tax	"	Special tax, frequently an excise tax on liquor or tobacco.	
Public Housing Authority (PHA)	"		Rent revenues plus taxing power of U.S. government through HUD.
Municipal notes	States, cities, towns, counties.		Often sold on discounted basis;

(cont.)

TABLE 5-1.   Continued

Type	Issuers	Backing	Types/Remarks
			maturities are based on need as interim financing.
Tax anticipation notes (TANs)	"	Proceeds of imminent tax collection.	"
Revenue anticipation notes (RANs)	"	Proceeds of imminent revenues.	"
Bond anticipation notes (BANs)	"	Proceeds of forthcoming bond issuance.	"
Project notes (PNs)	"	Refunded by long-term bonds.	Backed by full faith and credit of the U.S. government.

TRY THIS:

Which of the following is most likely to be backed by ad valorem taxes:
a. Industrial revenue bonds.
b. City general obligation bonds.
c. State general obligation bonds.
d. Special tax bonds.

HERE'S WHY:

The correct answer is (b). Ad valorem (real property) taxes are the usual backing for city bonds. Occasionally a city may have a city income and/or sales tax in addition to state levies. Such taxes, however, usually may be levied only with the prior approval of the state legislature.

Revenue bonds are issued by an agency, commission, or authority created by legislation to construct a "facility" such as a toll bridge, turnpike, hospital, or water, sewer, or electric system. Tolls, fees, or taxes are charged for use of the facility which ultimately pay off the debt. This type of bond is slightly riskier than GO bonds because they are not directly backed by the municipality; however, they generally pay a correspondingly higher coupon rate.

In some cases, especially with respect to sewer and electric system special assessment bonds, the underlying municipality or state assumes liability for the debt service if the income from the project is insufficient. Such issues are thus more like GOs than revenue bonds, and they are referred to as double-barreled issues.

Revenue bonds issued directly by the municipality, nonprofit authority, or other governmental unit to build a facility for a private corporation are called industrial development bonds (IDBs). A municipality issues a "tax-exempt" bond, builds a factory with the proceeds of the bond issue, then engages in a long-term lease agreement with an industrial corporation. The rent then passes through the authority to the bondholders as tax-exempt income. In effect, the corporation constructed a new plant at municipal borrowing rates which are lower than corporate borrowing rates due to the tax-free nature of the interest income. Recently, these issues have been restricted to those that improve civic services such as airports, harbors, mass transit, or pollution control facilities. The security behind this type of bond issue is the net lease entered into by the corporation and the issuer.

Special tax bonds are secured by the proceeds from a specific tax. This type of issue is frequently paid for by an excise tax on items such as liquor or tobacco. For example, a highway bond issue is paid out of gasoline taxes.

Public Housing Authority (PHA) bonds offer government backing to locally issued project bonds to assist in constructing low-income housing. The revenues (rents) are expected to pay the debt service, but if they do not, the full faith and credit of the U.S. government provides the ultimate security through the Housing and Urban Development Department (HUD). So investors get tax-exempt income, plus a government guarantee. Municipal notes—or project notes (PNs)—like these mature in one year or less and are issued under this arrangement for financing short-term projects.

TRY THIS:

A feasibility study and engineering reports would be *most* necessary prior to a new offering of
  I. General obligation bonds.
 II. Limited tax bonds.
III. Revenue bonds.

  a. I only.
  b. III only.
  c. II and III only.
  d. I and II only.

HERE'S WHY:

The correct answer is (b). Since the security for a revenue bond depends on the revenues produced by the use of the facilities (tolls on a turnpike, for example), engineering estimates of construction costs and potential traffic flow are critical. Engineering studies on the cost of, let's say, a new city hall to be built with the proceeds of a new general obligation bond would likewise be important but not as critical as with the revenues offering because of the taxing power of the issuer.

Municipal notes are short-term issues often sold on a discounted basis. Municipal bonds, on the other hand, pay interest semiannually. Municipal notes include

Tax anticipation notes (TANs), which are issued to raise monies securied by the proceeds of a forthcoming tax collection.

Revenue anticipation notes (RANs), which are issued to raise monies secured by the proceeds of future revenues.

Bond anticipation notes (BANs), which are issued as interim financing until a forthcoming bond issue is offered. The proceeds of the bond issue become the principal repayments for the BANs.

TANs, RANs, and BANs are sold on a discounted basis; therefore, the discount is the yield. Notes have no stated rate of return, so the profit realized from the difference between sale price and redemption value must be considered in the same category as interest payments on bonds, which are tax-free. The discount is considered tax-free income and not a capital gain or loss. Buyers are expected to hold notes to maturity, which leaves activity in the secondary market very low.

TRY THIS:

Which of the following are municipal obligations with maturities of less than one year?
  I. Treasury bills
 II. Project notes
III. Tax anticipation notes
IV. Certificates of deposit

a. I and IV only.
b. II and III only.
c. II, III, and IV only.
d. I, II, III, and IV.

HERE'S WHY:

The correct answer is (b). All four items listed are money market vehicles, but only the project notes and tax anticipation notes are municipal obligations. Other short-term municipals are bond anticipation notes and revenue anticipation notes.

The Risks of Municipal Bond Investment

Not all investment possibilities are without their risks, and municipals certainly have their share. The value of all bonds depends on interest rate fluctuations. When interest rates go up, bond prices usually fall. Another risk factor includes the possibility of whether the municipality will fail to pay the interest or principal on the bond when it matures. This rarely happens, but then again, anything can happen in the investment world.

When the credit rating of the municipality or the rating of its bonds is lowered, this may be the time to think about selling the bonds you may own. If the municipality is experiencing an economic crisis, the price of the bond should be checked often.

TRY THIS:

The credit rating of a municipality issuing bonds would be *least* affected by
a. Decline in assessed value of real estate.
b. Increase in capital spending projects.
c. Increase in welfare rolls.
d. Decrease in the prime interest rate.

HERE'S WHY:

The correct answer is (d). The prime interest rate is that charged a bank's most prestigious corporate clients. While it is an indicator of general credit conditions and can thus have an impact on municipal borrowings in an indirect sense, it is a short-term rate and would not affect a credit rating. Naturally a steep rise in the prime rate will also be reflected in higher interest rates for short-term municipal borrowings, like TANs, BANs, and RANs.

6
U.S. Government Securities

The Origin of Government Securities

The origin of government securities and debt is closely linked to the origin of the country itself. It can be said that the first U.S. government bond was issued as far back as 1790. In an effort to combine all the remaining debt from the Revolutionary War, the newly formed U.S. Treasury issued 4% notes that would mature in 10 years' time. And that was the beginning of what was to become the largest liquid capital market in the world.

Since that time, through many wars, debts, and repayments, the Treasury has made a regular habit of refunding existing debt and raising new money to finance the government's deficit. More and more is borrowed to pay off what was borrowed before. It's an endless cycle that manages to keep perpetuating itself.

Development of the Government Bond Market

Many of the early government bonds that were issued by the young U.S. Treasury Department were totally paid off. But by the time debts from the War of 1812 were run up, the amount was too high for the relatively new nation to bounce back from. Even though the amount of debt kept rising, investors knew that the government would not default on these loans, and they felt that government bonds were a safe haven for their hard-earned money. For much of the time, the New York Stock Exchange (NYSE) was the only available market for government bonds; there was no such thing as a *bond* market. Since these bonds were used more as a savings mechanism, trading volume on the NYSE was relatively low, and easily handled.

To handle the issuance of bonds, the U.S. Treasury originally appointed commercial banks to act as **distribution agents,** serving as both the **issuing agents** and the **primary buyers.** They were usually paid a commission of one-eighth of 1% for their services. At the same time, however, it was required that a national bank hold a certain amount of the securities. As a result, a liquid market wasn't really necessary since a portion of the available securities was guaranteed issuance. By the 1900s, institutional holders of these bonds were using brokers to execute the necessary services. In 1905, trading volume became so low that many of these brokers closed up shop or came close to it.

A turn of events that aided in the demise of the broker came about around 1911. **Dealer-banks** or first dealers started to offer customers commission-free handling of bond issues, which proved to be a very attractive offer. This changed again quickly enough when the Federal Reserve System was formed in 1913 and took over the issuance function of bonds for the Treasury. Dealers were left to handle the secondary market, which began to grow in its own right.

Well, as time went on, more and more unscrupulous dealers infiltrated the market, making a bad name for the reputable dealers and the market itself. In 1939, the Fed and the reputable dealers organized the Government Securities Dealer Group to regulate the growing government bond market. Under the watchful eye of the Fed via the primary dealers, who report to the New York Fed on a daily basis, this informal regulatory approach continues with the operations and executions of today. As a result of recent legislation, all dealers must be registered with a regulatory body and must adhere to the rules and regulations of the government bond market as set up by the Treasury Department.

Structure of the Marketplace

The government bond market is a very large telephone network set up for participants in the market to carry out the trading process. Trading rooms are set up throughout the United States and abroad and are designed to accommodate an **over-the-counter (OTC) market.**

This telephone network in a sometimes large, sometimes small, trading room can also be thought of as a huge wheel. The center of the wheel is where the Federal Reserve Bank is located. The Fed implements monetary policy through its Open Market Trading Desk and regulates the market participants. Fed brokers, equipped with telephones and other electronic equipment, communicate only with the primary dealers. Surrounding this central hub of activity are the primary dealers who communicate with other primary dealers, the Fed, customers, and of course, the brokers. Along the outer rim of this giant wheel are the customers. Transactions travel along the spokes of the wheel, moving away from and/or toward the center hub, from the broker, to the primary dealer, and ending with the customer.

The Over-the-Counter Market

The telephone network, or over-the-counter market, is basically an individual's market. One person (buyer) deals directly with one other person (seller) and negotiates the best price for the security.

Business is done as **principal,** which means that the broker/dealer is buying and selling for its own account. Therefore, it's going to make a transaction in its own best interest, not necessarily for the good of those being dealt with.

Who Plays What Roles?

Primary Dealer

As mentioned earlier, the OTC market works primarily on a one-to-one basis. The most visible part of this market is played by the **primary dealers.** They surround the hub of the giant wheel, communicating directly with the center, or Federal Reserve. Their responsibilities are many; one of them is to maintain liquid markets in all government and agency securities. A primary dealer must be ready at all times, day or night, to make markets and trade with any prospective and bona fide customer.

Another role of the primary dealer is to bid on all Treasury auctions for its own account and for its customer's account. The Fed monitors the dealer's aggressiveness and bids to make sure they meet their requirements.

Primary dealers must report to the Federal Reserve, on a daily basis, their securities positions, their trading volume, and their financing methods. This mandatory daily reporting process is how the government market is regulated.

There are three different types of primary dealers. They are commercial banks, full-service securities firms, and special-purpose government securities firms. Each of these has very special characteristics with special advantages and purposes. Commercial banks have a large supply of funds available for financing trading positions, and they have a customer base with which to trade. Full-service securities firms make most of their money from commissions as opposed to earning interest from loans, but they can execute transactions in corporate bonds and government bonds at the same time. Special-purpose government securities firms are not as numerous as years ago primarily because they have capital limitations and cannot trade corporate or foreign exchange bonds. They do still rely on a long-standing relationship with previous customers, which is what they tend to concentrate their trades on.

TRY THIS:

True or False? Dealers earn their income from the number of trades in one day.

HERE'S WHY:

This statement is False. Dealers earn their income from commissions on transactions they handle.

Brokers

Referring back to that giant wheel, brokers execute trades between the primary dealers, accepting commissions for their services. Since the Fed regulates all transactions and executions of the government bond market, the broker must deal accurately and honestly with the primary dealers. The brokers do not carry positions themselves, but solicit bids or offers from the primary dealers and relay that information to other primary dealers.

An important role of the broker is not to reveal the positions or trades of primary dealers to the other dealers. This avoids the unnecessary competition and jealousy that dealers can easily get carried away with.

Another important role of the broker is to provide the primary dealers with sources of information about the best bid or offer in any one security at any one time. Brokers have a network of computer terminals or CRT screens that are present in the offices of the primary dealers. These screens keep an up-to-date showing of the best bids and offers for each available security. This keeps the line of information open and current for all participating primary dealers.

TRY THIS:

True or False? A dealer's broker acts as an intermediary between prospective buying and selling firms.

HERE'S WHY:

This statement is True.

Customers

Government securities customers can be anyone doing business in these securities who is not a primary dealer or a broker. Customers generally fall into three different categories. The first is the **nonprimary dealer.** This is a firm that executes orders for its own customers. They can be either a commercial bank or a securities firm and sometimes directly compete with the primary dealers.

The second type of customer is the **leveraged investor** who buys and sells issues for his or her own account. Such customers are usually banks, thrifts, or trading firms. What sets these customers apart from the others is that they pay more for their money by issuing certificates of deposit or borrowing money to carry their securities than they can earn from a government bond with the same maturity. They assume that high interest rate risk will generate profits for them.

The third type of customer is the **unleveraged investor,** who oversees a pool of funds such as pension plans, insurance companies, mutual funds, and corporate cash portfolios to raise funds.

TRY THIS:

True or False? The public purchases U.S. Treasuries directly from the auction market.

HERE'S WHY:

This statement is False. On the OTC market, one person (buyer) deals directly with one other person (seller) and *negotiates* the best price for the security.

So, What Constitutes a Government Security?

As the bond market has changed over the years, with rising and falling interest rates and bond-quality variations, one thing that has remained fairly consistent is the dependability of U.S. government bonds. Not only is this market the largest, but it is also the most liquid capital market in the world.

However, as dependable as the government bond market has been, it still has experienced a number of changes. Long gone are the days where it was considered a small, stable market that dealt strictly with government bonds. It is now an enormous, volatile, and diverse market.

The demands of the financial system and the need for more capital have led to the increase of the overall size of the market. And the frequent rise and fall of interest rates have attributed to the market's volatility.

Besides government-issued bonds and securities, this market deals with securities issued by different agencies such as the Federal National Mortgage Association (FNMA), as well as certificates of deposit (CDs) issued by banks. They also trade mortgage-backed securities and Treasury notes and bills, not just bonds. So you see, because the investment climate has broadened its objectives and views, the respective investment markets have needed to change also to remain an active and successful part of this ever-changing environment.

Government Bond Categories

As the issuer of U.S. government securities, the Treasury Department is faced with the same financial problems that haunt most corporate finance officers. The Treasury Department is primarily responsible for paying the cost of operating the government.

The Treasury has the dual role of collective all revenues, through its Internal Revenue Service, and of paying all expenses through its General Accounting Office. These revenues and expenses are authorized by legislation passed by Congress and signed by the President.

If revenues match expenses, the budget is balanced. If expenses exceed revenues, the shortfall must be financed by the Treasury's issuing bills, notes, and/or bonds. Congress also sets the debt ceiling, which is binding on the Treasury—merely an agency of the government. If revenues exceed expenses, the resulting surplus is used to retire outstanding debt. (The last surplus in this country was 1969, under the Nixon administration, when we had a $1.8 billion surplus. Nixon, who is known and remembered for other things, shouldn't get exclusive credit for this surplus; he inherited a 10% war tax for Vietnam from the Johnson administration. Save that exception, we have had 28 straight deficits in a row culminating in over $200 billion deficits, now "down" to about $150 billion.)

Like corporations, the government often finds itself heavily in debt in order to pay for the way it wants to operate. There are three very broad categories that government debt falls into. They are

Nonmarketable.

Marketable.

Government-sponsored or government-agency obligations.

(See Table 6-1.)

Nonmarketable Securities

The most important nonmarketable securities issued by the U.S. government are **U.S. savings bonds.** These bonds are issued only in registered form, are payable only to the registered owner, and cannot be used as collateral for loans. Two types are currently being offered by the Treasury. They are the Series EE and Series HH savings bonds.

Series EE savings bonds help to provide a safe, yet convenient investment medium for the small investor. They are also protected against market price fluctuations. Interest compounds semiannually and is computed on a graduated scale until its maturity. If the bond is redeemed before it reaches maturity, a smaller interest rate is paid. The interest rate is periodically adjusted to maintain at least 85% of the yield on a five-year issue. The minimum rate is guaranteed at 7.5% if the bond is held five years or longer.

When the Treasury increases the interest rate on new issues, the rate is also increased on all outstanding issues. Therefore, if the interest rate increases during the time you own a bond, the amount you receive at maturity could be more than the face value of the bond.

Issued on a discount basis at 50% of face value, denominations of $50, $75, $100, $200, $500, $1000, $5,000, and $10,000 are available. Federal income tax is paid on income from these bonds when the bond is redeemed.

Series HH savings bonds are issued in denominations of $500, $1,000, $5,000, and $10,000. Though they are issued and redeemed at their par value, they cannot be redeemed until six months after they have been issued. Series HH bonds, which currently pay 7½% interest semiannually, have maturities of 10 years or longer. They are usually issued in exchange for Series E and EE bonds.

As with Series EE bonds, if the interest rate on new Series HH bonds is increased, payments on outstanding issues are also increased. As far as taxes go, the bond owner must pay federal income tax on any accumulated income earned on the bond when it is redeemed. However, the owner is exempt from paying any state or local income tax.

Retirement plan bonds are another form of nonmarketable security. The Treasury Department issued these bonds from January 1963 up until April 1982, only for those bond purchase plans connected with the Self-Employed Individuals' Tax Retirement Act of 1962. Issued in single ownership and beneficiary form, these bonds cannot be redeemed until the owner's death, disability, or attainment of age 59½.

The bonds were issued in denominations of $50, $100, $500, and $1,000, with a maximum purchase of $10,000 worth of bonds per calendar year. Interest varied from 3.75% to 9%, depending on the year of purchase, and was compounded semiannually. Principal, however, is payable only upon redemption of the bond. If the registered owner dies before the bond is redeemed, interest stops fives years after the death.

Once the bond is redeemed, the interest and principal are taxable as current income. However, the entire bond does not have to be redeemed at one time. Portions can be redeemed periodically when cash is needed, and to avoid large tax payments.

Other more obscure types of nonmarketable securities are **individual retirement bonds, government account series, depository bonds, state and local government series,** and **foreign series.**

TRY THIS:

Which of the following provides for increased payment on outstanding issues as the interest rate increases?
a. Commercial paper.
b. TANs.
c. Savings bonds.
d. T-bills.

HERE'S WHY:

The correct answer is (c). When the Treasury increases the interest rate on new issues, the rate is also increased on all outstanding issues. At maturity, you could, in essence, receive more than the face value of the bond if interest rates increase during your ownership of the bond.

TABLE 6-1. Summary of U.S. Government Securities.

	Market-able	Denominations	Maturities	Interest	Quotations	Form	Remarks
Series EE	No	$50–$1,000	Varies with rate	Minimum 7½%	NA	Registered	Maximum purchase of $15,000 (purchase price) in one year
Series HH	No	$500–$5,000	10 years	7½%	NA	Registered	
Treasury bills	Yes	$10,000 to $1 million	13 weeks, 26 weeks, and 52 weeks	Varies per competitive bidding	Bid and asked percentages, always at a discount	Book entry	Cash management bills are T bills, e.g., bid: 13⅛ Asked: 13¼%
Treasury notes	Yes	$1,000 to $1 million	1 to 10 years	Per indenture	Percentage of face value	Registered	
Treasury bonds	Yes	$500 to $1 million	5 to 35 years	Fixed per indenture	Bid and asked plus current yield and yield to maturity	Registered	Term bonds are T-bonds with call provision. Flower T-bonds no longer issued, e.g., Bid: 74¾ Asked: 75¼ Current yield: 7.65% Yield-to-maturity: 8.52%
Federal Home Loan Banks (Freddie Mac)	Yes	Short-term discount notes (minimum $50,000	30 to 270 days	Discount from face value periodically set		Book entry	

Issuer		Instrument / Denomination	Maturity	Interest	Pricing	Form	Callable
Government National Mortgage Association (Ginnie Mae)	Yes	Debentures: $10,000 to $500,000	3 to 25 years	Per indenture	Percentage of face value	Book entry	Usually noncallable
		Mortgage-backed bonds ($25,000)	10 to 30 years	Per indenture	Percentage of face value	Bearer or registered	
		Participation certificates ($5,000 minimum)	1 to 25 years	Per indenture		Registered	
		Passthrough certificates ($25,000 and up in $5,000 increments)	20 to 30 years	Per indenture	Percentage of face value	Registered	
Federal National Mortgage Association (Fannie Mae) Debentures	Yes	$10,000, increments of $5,000 thereafter	2 to 25 years	Per indenture	Percentage of face value	Book entry	
Federal National Mortgage Association (Fannie Mae) short-term notes	Yes	$5,000 to $1 million	30 to 360 days	Varies competitively	Discounted yield	Book entry	Minimum order $50,000

Marketable Securities

After a U.S. government obligation is originally issued (through a Federal Reserve Bank), it is freely traded in the secondary market. These obligations are called **marketable securities.**

Marketable securities, namely, Treasury bills, notes, and bonds, make up the largest securities market in the world. Even though the U.S. government has no demonstrable means of repaying debts or any collateral to speak of, it has become the number one issuer of debt securities. The Treasury issues securities that have maturities ranging from a few days to 30 years. Some of their key points are discussed in the paragraphs that follow.

Treasury bills have maturities ranging up to one year where the Federal Reserve issues three-month and six-month bills at a weekly auction and one-year bills at a monthly auction. They are issued in book-entry form, which means that records of the purchase are held on the books of the Treasury Department. The owner receives only a receipt of the purchase, never an actual bond certificate stating ownership.

These bills are always sold at a discount from face value and yet are redeemed at face value. The amount of discount (the difference between the actual price paid for the bond and the amount received at maturity) determines the rate of interest received by the investor. This rate of return is expressed as a bond equivalent yield. A T-bill has no nominal yield.

For example, investor Jones buys a $100,000, 13-week bill priced at a discount of 10%. She pays approximately $97,500 for the T-bill. After 13 weeks, she redeems it for $100,000. The $2,500 difference represents interest of $10,000 annually. If Jones held a $100,000, 10% debt instrument for one full year, she would be paid $10,000 in interest ($100,000 times 10%). Since she held the bill for only a quarter of a year, she is entitled to a quarter of the annual interest ($10,000 times .25), or $2,500.

Given the discount in dollars, you can calculate the yield, which is simply the discount expressed as a percentage. To make this computation, dealers use the actual number of days to maturity based on a theoretical 360-day year:

$$\begin{matrix} \text{Discount} \\ \text{(per \$100 of} \\ \text{maturity value)} \end{matrix} = \frac{\text{Days to maturity}}{360} \times \text{Rate (\%)}$$

To find the price, use the following formula:

Price ($) = $100 − discount (per $100 of maturity value)

As an example, let's find the dollar price for a T-bill that is due in 147 days and trades on a 9% discount basis.

$$D = M \div 360 \times R \ (\%)$$
$$= 147 \div 360 \times .09$$
$$= 3.6750\% \ \text{full discount}$$

In other words, the investor receives a discount of $3.675 per $100 of maturity value. For a $100,000 bill, the discount is $3,675.00 ($3,675 times 1,000).

The next step is to calculate the price:

$$P = \$100 - D$$
$$= \$100 - \$3.675 \ \text{per} \ \$100$$
$$= \$96.325$$

The dollar price of the T-bill is equal to $96.325 for every $100 of face (or redemption) value. So, a $100,000 bill sold on a 9% basis would cost $96,325.00 and be redeemed for $100,000 after 147 days.

The discount is the pricing mechanism for T-bills.

EXAMPLE:

A discount of 12% on a one-year bill would produce a price of 88 (100 − 12), but the same discount on a 13-week bill would produce a price of 97 [100 − (12 ÷ 4)] (It matures in a quarter of a year.) The yield on each of these bills would be higher than the discount rate because the buyer received the discount rate on less than the par amount of cash. Thus, the yield on this hypothetical year bill would be 13.64% (12% ÷ .88), and the yield on the 13-week bill would be 12.37% (12% ÷ .97).

Let's take a look at Figure 6-1. On March 6, a T-bill with a face value of $100,000 and a maturity of September 4 is quoted as follows:

	Bid	Asked	Yield
Discount	6.61%	6.59%	6.91%
Dollar price	$96,695	$96,705	

The asked dollar price ($96,705) was computed as follows, using 180 days as the time between March 6 and September 4.

$$\text{Discount} = M \div 360 \times R \times \text{face value}$$
$$= 180 \div 360 \times .0659 \times \$100,000$$
$$= \$3,295$$

$$\text{Price (\$)} = \text{Face value discount}$$
$$= \$100,000 - \$3,295$$
$$= \$96,705$$

The Treasury generally issues bills in three maturities: 13 weeks, 26 weeks, and 52 weeks. They are also known as the "three-month

U.S. Treas. Bills

Mat. date -1989-	Bid	Asked	Yield Discount	Mat. date -1989-	Bid	Asked	Yield Discount
3-13	5.52	5.38	5.46	7-10	6.70	6.66	6.91
3-20	6.12	6.04	6.13	7-17	6.70	6.66	6.92
3-27	5.67	5.55	5.64	7-24	6.70	6.66	6.93
4- 3	6.19	6.13	6.24	7-86	6.70	6.68	6.97
4-10	6.14	6.08	6.20	8- 7	6.78	6.74	7.03
4-17	6.44	6.40	6.53	8-14	6.69	6.65	6.94
4-24	6.46	6.40	6.54	8-21	6.70	6.66	6.96
5- 1	6.61	6.55	6.70	8-28	6.68	6.64	6.95
5- 8	6.68	6.64	6.81	9- 4	6.61	6.59	6.91
5-15	6.68	6.66	6.83	10- 2	6.67	6.63	6.96
5-22	6.67	6.63	6.81	10-30	6.67	6.63	6.97
5-29	6.71	6.67	6.87	11-28	6.68	6.64	7.00
6- 5	6.61	6.59	6.79	12-26	6.66	6.62	7.00
6-12	6.60	6.56	6.77	-1988-			
6-19	6.65	6.61	6.83	1-22	6.66	6.64	7.04
6-26	6.51	6.45	6.67	2-19	6.63	6.61	7.04
7- 3	6.70	6.66	6.90				

FIGURE 6-1.   T-bill quotations.

bill," "six-month bill," and the "year bill," although they conform to those time periods for only one day.

Bills are traditionally purchased and traded by large investors, either institutions or very wealthy individuals. They are also traded in very large volume. At least half of each day's trading volume in the Treasury securities markets is in bills, approximately $10 billion each day. In addition, each individual transaction is usually very large. In fact, the usual round lot in the bill market is $5 million. Bills are issued in amounts as small as $100,000, but those amounts are considered odd lots in the market, and they trade at decidedly detrimental prices when compared to round lots.

Treasury bills are sold in denominations of $10,000 up to $1 million in increments of $5,000. For this reason, they are not suitable for the small investor.

TRY THIS:

A Treasury bill is sold at a discount basis which determines its
a. Face value.
b. Rate of return.
c. Nominal yield.
d. Yield to call.

HERE'S WHY:

The correct answer is (b). The amount of discount—the difference between what investors pay at the discounted purchase price and the face value they receive at maturity—determines the rate of interest received on this investment. Bills are always sold at a discount from face value and always redeemed at full face value. The discount determines the rate of return, expressed as a bond equivalent yield. A T-bill has no nominal yield.

Treasury notes have maturities ranging from a few days to 10 years and are issued in either registered form or book-entry form. They carry a fixed rate of interest and are issued, quoted, and traded as a percentage of their face value.

Notes are the second largest type of security that is issued by the

U.S Treasury. They are issued with maturities ranging from 1 year to 10 years. Unlike bills, Treasury notes have coupons and pay interest twice a year: once on the anniversary of the maturity date and once again six months later. Interest rates range from $6\frac{1}{8}$% to $16\frac{1}{4}$%. Another differing point is that notes cannot be called by the Treasury Department during the life of the note. In recent years, notes have been issued in registered form, where interest is paid out to holders of record by the Federal Reserve. Banks keep records of ownership of their customers and keep track of payments credited to these customers' accounts.

Notes are issued in the same regular manner that bills are issued, though not quite as frequently. They follow a different maturity cycle known as **quarterly refunding.** Quarterly refundings occur in the months of February, May, August, and November. Though the notes are issued in these four months, the process begins already the month before. On the last Wednesday of January, April, July, and October, the Treasury announces the sizes and maturities of the issues to be sold the following week. These issues will be delivered on the fifteenth day of February, May, August, and November. The issuance of the new notes partly refunds the ones that are still maturing and partly raises the new money the Treasury needs to borrow. As the Treasury's borrowing needs grew, more cycles were added. This **minirefunding** occurs in March, June, September, and December. Some of the Treasury's note cycles might look like the following:

The 2-year note—auctioned monthly, toward the end of the month, is delivered on the last business day of the month. Matures two years later, on the delivery date.

The 4-year note—auctioned in March, June, September, and December as part of the minirefunding.

The 10-year note—auctioned in February, May, August, and November as part of the quarterly refunding.

Denominations of notes can range from $1,000 to $500 million, carrying a fixed rate of interest. They are issued, quoted, and traded at a percentage of their face value. The percentage point can be broken down as far as thirty-seconds of a point, and sometimes even as far as sixty-fourths of a point. For example, if a price is quoted as 96.16, it would be read as $96\frac{1}{2}$% of par, or $965,000 per million dollars par amount. A million-dollar par amount is considered a round lot in the note market.

Many commercial banks, Federal Reserve banks, U.S. government agencies, and trust funds own Treasury notes and stagger their maturity dates so that varying financial requirements can be met over a number of years.

TRY THIS:

Which of the following is an intermediate-debt instrument of the federal government, issued in coupon or interest rate form?
a. Limited tax bond.
b. Treasury note.
c. Treasury bill.
d. Municipal bond.

HERE'S WHY:

The correct answer is (b). Treasury notes are federal registered or bearer obligations issued in denominations of $1,000 to $500 million for maturities of 1 to 10 years, carrying a fixed rate of interest. These notes are issued, quoted, and traded at a percentage of their face value.

Treasury bonds can have any maturity, but it is usually 5 to 35 years. They are available in registered or book-entry form, which are interchangeable. If the bond owner wants to transfer a registered bond to a book-entry form, for example, the Treasury Department does so one month before each interest payment date.

Treasury bonds carry a fixed interest rate and are issued, quoted, and traded as a percentage of their face value. They are offered in denominations of $500 up to $1 million, but are usually issued in $1,000 denominations.

If a Treasury bond carries a call feature in the indenture, which allows the government to redeem the bond before maturity, the bond is called a **term bond** and the yield is calculated to the call date. The Treasury Department rarely uses its call privilege.

Some bonds are callable by the Treasury at 100, five years before they mature. Thus you can assume that, if a bond is trading substantially above 100, it may well have a maturity five years shorter than the stated one. That change in maturity can affect the bond's price performance, making it less volatile than it otherwise would be.

Several years ago, Congress passed a law stating that the Treasury cannot issue bonds that yield more than $4\frac{1}{4}\%$. For many years, that meant that the Treasury has effectively been prevented from issuing bonds. Rather than repeal the law, Congress has chosen to give the Treasury limited authority to issue bonds yielding more than $4\frac{1}{4}\%$. As the Treasury's appetite for money has grown, it has had to go back to Congress again and again for more authority. Occasionally when Congress and the current administration are at a political standoff, Congress witholds the bond authority.

Generally, the Treasury has two bond cycles:

1. The 20-year bond—auctioned in March, June, September, and December as part of the minirefunding.
2. The 30-year bond—auctioned in February, May, August, and November as part of the quarterly refunding.

The fact that T-bonds can be easily and quickly converted to cash at a low transaction price is reflected by the slight "spread" between the bid and the asked prices, though often very small. Treasury bonds are, like T-notes, quoted in thirty-seconds of a point. For example, a $1,000 government bond is quoted at 96.6. This quotation means $96\frac{6}{32}\%$ of the bond's par value. The price is figured as follows:

$$96 = 96\% \text{ of par value} \qquad \$960.000$$
$$.6 = \frac{6}{32} \text{ or } (\frac{3}{16}) \text{ of } \$10 \qquad + \quad 1.875$$
$$\text{Dollar price} \qquad\qquad \$961.875$$

TRY THIS:

Which of the following are discount instruments?
a. U.S. Treasury bills.
b. U.S. Treasury bonds.
c. CDs.
d. Treasury stock.

HERE'S WHY:

The correct answer is (a). A Treasury bill is a federal bearer obligation issued in denominations of \$10,000 to \$1 million with a maturity date usually of three months to one year. It is fully marketable at a discount from face value (which determines the interest rate).

T-bonds are quoted in the financial news. Price quotations are given for every hundred dollars of face value. The first column in the quotations listing shown in Figure 6-2 shows the original rate

TREASURY BONDS, NOTES & BILLS

Representative mid-afternoon Over-the-Counter quotations supplied by the Federal Reserve Bank of New York City, based on transactions of \$1 million or more.

Decimals in bid-and-asked and bid changes represent 32nds; 101.1 means $101\frac{1}{32}$. a-Plus $\frac{1}{64}$. b-Yield to call date. d-Minus $\frac{1}{64}$. k-Nonresident aliens exempt from withholding taxes. n-Treasury notes. p-Treasury note; nonresident aliens exempt from withholding taxes.

Treasury Bonds and Notes

Rate	Mat. Date	Bid	Asked	Bid Chg.	Yld.
14s,	1986 Mar n	100.11	100.15	− 1	5.13
11 1/2s,	1986 Mar n	100.7	100.11	...	4.97
11 3/4s,	1986 Apr n	100.19	100.23	...	6.24
7 7/8s,	1986 May n	100.3	100.7	+ .1	6.48
9 3/8s,	1986 May n	100.11	100.15	...	6.54
12 5/8s,	1986 May n	101.4	101.8	− .1	6.43
13 3/4s,	1986 May n	101.3	101.7	...	6.83
13s,	1986 Jun n	101.22	101.26	...	6.79
14 7/8s,	1986 Jun n	102.8	102.12	− .1	6.77
12 5/8s,	1986 Jul p	102.2	102.6	...	6.81
8s,	1986 Aug n	100.10	100.14	+ .1	6.92
11 3/8s,	1986 Aug n	101.24	101.28	+ .1	6.87
12 3/8s,	1986 Aug p	102.11	102.15	...	6.93
11 7/8s,	1986 Sep p	102.15	102.19	...	7.03
12 1/4s,	1986 Sep n	102.22	102.26	+ .1	7.00
11 3/8s,	1986 Oct p	102.21	102.25	...	7.10
6 1/8s,	1986 Nov	99.21	100.21	+ .3	5.13
10 3/8s,	1986 Nov p	102.3	102.7	+ .2	7.18
11s,	1986 Nov n	102.12	102.16	+ .1	7.18
13 7/8s,	1986 Nov n	104.10	104.14	+ .2	7.09
16 1/8s,	1986 Nov n	105.24	105.28	...	7.14
9 7/8s,	1986 Dec p	101.31	102.3	+ .1	7.16
10s,	1986 Dec n	102.1	102.5	...	7.21
9 3/4s,	1987 Jan p	102.1	102.5	+ .1	7.22
9s,	1987 Feb n	101.12	101.18	...	7.24
10s,	1987 Feb p	102.13	102.17	+ .2	7.25
10 7/8s,	1987 Feb n	103.3	103.7	+ .1	7.25
12 3/4s,	1987 Feb n	104.29	105.1	...	7.09
10 1/4s,	1987 Mar n	102.30	103.2	+ .3	7.19
10 3/4s,	1987 Mar p	103.13	103.17	+ .2	7.22
9 3/4s,	1987 Apr p	102.18	102.22	+ .2	7.25
9 1/8s,	1987 May p	102	102.4	+ .2	7.28
12s,	1987 May n	105.5	105.9	+ .3	7.26
12 1/2s,	1987 May n	105.22	105.26	+ .3	7.28
14s,	1987 May n	107.11	107.15	+ .2	7.29
8 1/2s,	1987 Jun p	101.14	101.18	+ .2	7.23
10 1/2s,	1987 Jun n	103.26	103.30	+ .1	7.29
8 7/8s,	1987 Jul p	101.30	102.2	+ .4	7.29
8 7/8s,	1987 Aug p	102.2	102.6	+ .5	7.28
12 3/8s,	1987 Aug p	106.20	106.24	+ .4	7.33
13 3/4s,	1987 Aug n	108.15	108.19	+ .4	7.33
9s,	1987 Sep p	102.12	102.16	+ .5	7.27
11 1/8s,	1987 Sep n	105.15	105.19	+ .5	7.26
8 7/8s,	1987 Oct p	102.6	102.10	+ .1	7.35
7 5/8s,	1987 Nov n	100.11	100.19	+ .6	7.24
8 1/2s,	1987 Nov p	101.25	101.29	+ .4	7.30
11s,	1987 Nov p	105.17	105.21	+ .4	7.36
12 5/8s,	1987 Nov n	107.31	108.3	+ .2	7.42
11 1/4s,	1987 Dec n	106.12	106.16	+ .3	7.35
7 7/8s,	1987 Dec p	100.22	100.26	+ .2	7.39
8 1/8s,	1988 Jan p	101.8	101.10	+ .5	7.37
12 3/8s,	1988 Jan n	108.12	108.16	+ .2	7.38
10 1/8s,	1988 Feb n	104.24	104.28	+ .2	7.38
10 3/8s,	11988 Feb p	105.6	105.10	+ .4	7.38
8s,	1988 Feb p	101.9	101.11	+ .5	7.26
12s	1988 Mar n	108.18	108.22	+ .6	7.37
13/4s,	1988 Apr n	111.2	111.6	+ .6	7.39
8 1/4s,	1988 May n	101.24	102	+ .5	7.24
9 7/8s,	1988 May n	104.24	104.28	+ .7	7.41
10s,	1988 May p	105.1	105.5	+ .4	7.40
13 5/8s,	1988 Jun n	112.20	112.24	+ .4	7.51
14s	1988 Jul n	113.17	113.25	+ .3	7.50

FIGURE 6-2. Treasury Bond Quotations

with an "s" after it to make the pronunciation easier. For example, a 14% bond due in 1986 is called "fourteens of eighty-six."

The next two columns give the year and month of maturity. An "n" designates a note whereas all the other listings refer to bonds. Securities are listed in chronological order with earlier-maturing issues listed first and newer issues listed later. Issues designated with a "p" are exempt from withholding tax if they are held by non-U.S. citizens.

The next group of columns indicate, first, the midafternoon bid price at which the dealers were willing to buy the issue. The second column gives the asked, or dealer selling, price. The next column gives the changes in the bid price from the previous day. The last column gives the yield, or effective return on the investment. This calculation takes into account the original interest rate, the current asked price, and the amount of time left until the bond or note reaches maturity.

TRY THIS:

Bonds are issued with maturities ranging from
a. 1–10 years.
b. 10–20 years.
c. 20–30 years.
d. 5–35 years.

HERE'S WHY:

The correct answer is (d). Treasury bonds are federal registered or bearer obligations issued in denominations of $500 to $1 million with maturities ranging from 5 to 35 years, carrying a fixed interest rate and issued, quoted, and traded as a percentage of its face value.

LET'S TRY ANOTHER ONE:

All the following securities are marketable except
a. Tax anticipation bills.
b. Term bonds.
c. Ginnie Maes.
d. Series EE bonds.

HERE'S WHY:

The correct answer is (d). The Treasury Department sells and redeems two securities directly to the public: Series EE savings bonds and Series HH bonds. The Series EE bonds are registered securities offered in various denominations (minimum $50) at one-half of their face value and redeemed at face value at maturity.

The Origin of Agency Securities

Stop and thing for a moment where this nation would be if it weren't for the family farmer. Through the years that this nation fought for its freedom, the farmer, the strong base of support and nourishment in earlier days, became almost a heroic figure in relation to the foundation of this country. Therefore, the individual farmer's successes and plights became a very important part of what Americans believed in. Think also of the family homeowner. Every hard-working American's dream was to own a home.

What does the farmer and homeowner have to do with agency securities? The farmer, who operates in a "lowest-price" market, is not a very efficient producer of commodities. The homeowner, who is dependent on long-term debts, subjects his or her lender to high interest rate risk. What if general interest rates rise during the term of a 20-year mortgage? The lending bank is "stuck" with a loan that pays at rates lower than those currently available.

Because of the economic uncertainty involved in both these cases, the government felt that intervention was needed in the form of low-cost loans to farmers and homeowners. However, it was not fair, it was decided, for the government to interfere with the economic process, especially when certain groups would appear to benefit from such intervention. Hence, the organization of federal agencies.

A federal agency, which can be considered a cross between a government body and a private corporation, is usually owned by the particular industry it benefits. The agency helps to regulate that industry.

Agencies are usually divided into two categories:

1. **Those that assist the farming sector:** the Federal Intermediate Credit Banks, the Banks for Cooperatives, and the Federal Land Banks.

2. **Those that assist the homeownership sector:** the Federal National Mortgage Association, the Federal Home Loan Banks, the Federal Home Loan Mortgage Corporation, and the Government National Mortgage Association.

Two other agencies occasionally issue or guarantee securities: the Export-Import Bank and the Tennessee Valley Authority. These agencies, however, represent a very small part of the market.

Agencies operate in one of two ways. One way is to borrow money in the marketplace by issuing securities and lending the proceeds to their owners/constituents. This enables them to substitute their high-quality credit for the lower-quality credit of the farmer or homeowner.

Another way is to guarantee the payment of principal and interest on bonds issued by their owner/constituents. Some agencies do both, and some include the good credit of the Treasury. Either way, they are considered a stable means of investment.

Agency Notes and Debentures

Agency securities fall into two classes regarding issuance. Direct agency issues use a procedure that falls between a Treasury auction and a corporate underwriting, while mortgage-backed securities are issued in a totally uncontrolled process. Direct agency issues are handled by each agency's fiscal agent, who occupies a position similar to that of a corporate treasurer. Unlike the Treasury, agencies pay the primary dealers (and a few other participants) a commission to market their securities, giving the dealers an exclusive franchise to do this job. The dealers know ahead of time which agency will be issuing securities and when. They vie with each other to market the largest amount of securities for each agency, thereby hoping to increase their allotment and the resulting total commission.

The mortgage-backed securities (MBSs) differ from the issuance of Treasuries of direct issue agencies in the following manner. Instead of an announced issue or auction by a centralized entity, MBSs are sold by each of the originating mortgage bankers, without any control by the guaranteeing agency. They are often sold many months before they are delivered and before they even exist.

The Farm Credit Agencies

The **Banks for Cooperatives,** or **Co-Op,** is a cooperatively owned system of banks and associations that provide mortgage loans to eligible farmers nationwide. Even though Banks for Cooperatives are operated under federal charter and are government-supervised, the government assumes no direct or indirect liability for their debentures.

These bonds are issued only in book-entry form, in denominations of $5,000, $10,000, $50,000, and $100,000. Interest is subject to federal income tax, but is exempt from state and local income and property taxes.

The **Federal Intermediate Credit Banks (FICBs)** were created to provide a dependable source of funds for institutions that lend to farmers. One bank was established in each of the 12 Farm Credit districts to operate under the supervision of the Farm Credit Administration. These banks serve primarily as discount banks for institutions that finance agricultural and livestock products, including the production credit associations organized under the Farm Credit Act of 1933. The banks may also make direct loans to qualified farm financial institutions, and they provide supervisory services to the production credit associations upon request.

The **Federal Land Bank** system was created in each of the 12 farm districts across the country. The Federal Farm Credit Act of 1933 transferred control of the Federal Land Banks to the newly created Farm Credit Administration, and the farm districts became known as Farm Credit districts. Although the banks are operated under the close supervision of the Farm Credit Administration, they are now wholly owned by farmers through local Federal Land Bank associations.

The Federal Land Bank's function is to make long-term first mortgage loans on farm properties within each of the 12 farm districts. Such loans were originally made directly to the farmer, but they are now closed through one of the nearly 700 local associations. These loans may not exceed 65% of the appraised value of the land mortgaged as security, and the local association must endorse each loan note.

Although the farm credit agencies used to issue separate securities, they now issue only under the umbrella of the Federal Farm Credit System. Like many corporations, the Farm Credit System borrows short-term money on a regular basis. The system issues discount notes, which are the agency equivalent of Treasury bills. Unlike bills, however, these notes are not sold at auction, but are sold to dealers, and by dealers to customers, as the system needs to raise money.

The Farm Credit System has regular issuance of six-month and nine-month bonds through the selling group. These issues are such a regular event that they are comparable to the Treasury refundings. Their liquidity is fairly high in the week or two after they are issued, but it gradually decreases and then drops off sharply when the next six- and nine-month bonds are issued. Then the old bonds become "off-the-run" securities, signifying that they have much less liquidity and trading volume than the active issues.

All Farm Credit System securities are issued in book-entry form only, which means that the buyers do not receive certificates. Instead, their ownership is recorded on the computers at their clearing banks and at the Federal Reserve. Interest and principal payments are made based on those computer records, not on presentation of a coupon or certificate.

Regarding tax treatment, interest on Farm Credit securities is exempt from state and local income taxes, but not from federal income tax. Gains from sale, transfer, or inheritance of these securities are subject to federal, state, and local taxes.

TRY THIS:

True or False? The U.S. government assumes no direct or indirect liability for Co-ops.

HERE'S WHY:

This statement is True. Initially, the Banks for Cooperatives were wholly owned by the U.S. government, but the Farm Credit Act of 1955 provided for the gradual retirement of the government's investment and conversion to private ownership. The last of the government's capital stock was retired by December 31, 1968, and the banks are now wholly owned by the private cooperative associations they serve.

Mortgage Credit Agencies

Three mortgage credit agencies have developed over the years since the Great Depression. They are

1. The **Federal Home Loan Bank (FHLB)** system oversees the federally chartered thrift institutions in the United States and helps them in fulfilling their mortgage lending responsibilities.
2. The **Federal National Mortgage Association (FNMA)** provides direct assistance to the market for conventional mortgages.
3. The **Government National Mortgage Association (GNMA)** provides assistance to the market for federally insured mortgages.

Both the FHLB and FNMA issue securities directly, and all three guarantee issues of mortgage passthrough securities.

The Federal Home Loan Bank (FHLB) system was organized and opened for business in 1932. The 12 district banks that make up this system encourage the financing of residential construction in this country. Known as "Freddie Macs," these bonds are not directly backed by the taxing power of the federal government; however, the Treasury is authorized to buy up to $4 billion of these securities. Cash, securities, and other bank assets are used as collateral.

These debts are issued in bearer form in denominations of $10,000, $50,000, $100,000, and $1,000,000. Interest is subject to federal income taxes but is exempt from state and local income and property taxes.

The Federal National Mortgage Association (FNMA) buys mortgages approved by the Federal Housing Administration (FHA), Veterans Administration (VA), and Farmers Home Administration (FHDA), as well as conventional mortgages. It is a government-sponsored, publicly owned corporation that was established to provide liquidity for mortgage investments. The corporation purchases mortgages when the supply of mortgage funds are low and sells mortgages when the supply of funds are high.

The FNMA, or "Fannie Mae," issues bonds in bearer form only and in denominations of $10,000 and $5,000 increments. Interest is subject to all federal and local taxes.

When the FNMA became publicly owned, the Government National Mortgage Association (GNMA) took its place as a wholly owned government corporation. "Ginnie Mae" bonds are fully backed by the federal government, but their interest payments are not exempt from state and local taxes.

GNMA bonds provide investors with monthly interest payments instead of semiannual and are issued in registered form. These bonds are issued in denominations of $25,000 and reach maturity in 10 to 30 years.

When FNMA was converted to private ownership in 1968, all its outstanding participation certificates were transferred to GNMA's Management and Liquidating Functions Division.

All participation certificates issues by FNMA or GNMA are guaranteed by GNMA as to both principal and interest. These certificates do not carry any guarantee by the government, although the Secretary of the Treasury would make any loans necessary to GNMA to enable it to meet its obligations.

Each issue of these participation certificates was issued through a syndicate of underwriting dealers. The certificates are not callable. The early issues were available only in registered form, but the later issues were registered at the option of the buyer. Most issues offered denominations of $5,000, $10,000, $25,000, $100,000, $500,000, and $1,000,000. Interest is payable semiannually.

Mortgage-Backed Passthrough Securities

The growth in mortgage-backed passthrough securities in the government securities market has been spectacular. During the late 1960s the thrift industry, which had been the primary source of single-family mortgages, was subject to too many pressures and fluctuations to be depended upon to supply the necessary funds. With the creation of GNMA in 1968 came an entirely new security, a cross between a publicly traded bond and a single-family mortgage. It was a security, like a note or bond, representing an interest in a pool of mortgages and was guaranteed by GNMA. They were called mortgage-backed passthrough securities because they were backed by federally insured single-family mortgages, on which the principal and interest payments were "passed through" to the holder of the security. The actual issuer of the MBS is a mortgage banker. The mortgage banker services all the loans in the pool, collecting the individual monthly payments and passing the funds along, less a servicing fee, 45 days later.

Within the first five years of the 1980s, both the Federal Home Loan Mortgage Corporation (FHLMC) and FNMA began to issue and guarantee MBSs. Theirs, however, are backed by conventional mortgages, and their guarantees do not incorporate the full faith and credit of the Treasury. As you might expect, their securities carry a higher market yield than do GNMAs, and the market is less liquid. But both the markets are growing all the time.

Because of their mortgagelike nature, the market for passthrough securities has some distinct differences from the market for other debt securities. Traditionally, mortgage trades have been done for settlement several months in the future, when the mortgages are available for delivery. Passthrough securities are traded for settlement from a few days to six months in the future, with the wide majority settling from one to three months after the trade.

Stripped Securities and OIDs

Another recent introduction to the area of government securities is the **stripped** issue. This is where the interest coupons of Treasury bonds are separated or "stripped" from the principal amount. Proceeds from the sale of the parts of the original issue are usually greater than the market value of the issue if it were sold intact. This type of security can be very complicated because it allows so many varieties of issues. A specific issue, for example, could sell with or without interest payments for the life of the security or at vastly different prices.

Original issue discounts (OIDs) are securities issued with a coupon below the market interest rate and with a price below 100. OIDs are not a favorite choice of taxable accounts because the discount paid for the issue must be amortized over the life of the issue, and taxes must be paid on it. Pension funds and other investors who do not have to pay taxes usually invest in this type of security.

Derivative Products

To solve the ever-increasing problem of interest rate volatility, dealers had to find a way to ease the high risk they faced and to avoid the shortages of capital that stimulated this high volatility of interest rates. The answer turned out to be in investment products that relied on other instruments for price performance. Two of the more common derivative products are **financial futures** and **debt options.**

A **futures contract** is an agreement to make or take delivery of a commodity at a specified future time and price. Originally, the commodity was often just a bulk good such as grains or precious metals, but now it includes financial instruments, currencies, and indexes. Financial futures, in particular, are contracts to receive or deliver securities such as Treasury bills, Treasury bonds, foreign currencies, GNMAs, or certificates of deposit.

The futures market allows the investor to transfer the risk of long- or short-term securities to those who are willing to take on those risks. This method of reducing risk is often referred to as **hedging.** For example, if investors expect interest rates to rise, investing in futures can offset the decline in the value of their assets during this period.

The debt option is a contract wherein the option writer (or seller) grants the option buyer (or holder) the right to demand that the writer perform a certain act. This act could be to *call;* that is, the buyer can purchase from the seller a security or commodity for a fixed price during a certain period of time. Or it could be to *put;* that is, the buyer can sell a security at a set price during a set period of time. When the price of a security rises, the call option buyer benefits; when the price falls, the put option buyer benefits.

There are many options strategies that investors can work out to their best advantage in order to manage and improve interest rate risk, investment return, and other volatile characteristics inherent in a bond portfolio.

7

Money Market Instruments

The Money Market

Before the late 1970s and early 1980s, most individuals were content to leave their ready cash in the local bank or savings and loan (S&L). In effect, they lent it to the bank, which in turn lent it to borrowers at a higher rate. After all, the bank offered safety, paid between 4% and 5¼% interest, and offered immediate liquidity.

The relative attractiveness of putting surplus cash into the bank changed in the late 1970s and early 1980s as interest rates skyrocketed. The combination of high inflation, the rapid rise in oil prices, and the tight money policies enacted by the Federal Reserve Board all combined to push short-term interest rates up over 20%. Even financially strong borrowers were willing to pay more than 20% a year to borrow money.

Unfortunately for investors, banks and S&Ls were legally restricted from paying their depositors an interest rate higher than 5¼%. To many investors this seemed unfair. After all, if borrowers were willing to pay 20% a year and you had money to lend, why settle for 5¼%?

Soon investors found a number of vehicles that offered sharply higher interest rates but that also required substantially higher minimum investments (often exceeding $100,000). Since this was more than most people could afford to invest, many investors could not take advantage of the higher rates offered by these vehicles.

To solve this problem, many mutual fund companies started offering money market mutual funds. In these money funds investors could pool their resources, hire a professional manager, and enjoy the higher rates of return offered by the so-called "money market." As the popularity of these money market funds spread, more and more people withdrew their money from banks and S&Ls, creating a severe liquidity crisis for many banks and S&Ls.

Although many investors bought (and are still buying) shares in money market funds, few really understand the vehicles that make up the money market.

Money Market Vehicles

Traditionally, money market vehicles are defined as relatively risk-free debt securities that mature in less than a year. Included in this definition are

Commercial paper (CP).

Banker's acceptances (BAs).

Most negotiable ($100,000 and over) certificates of deposit (CDs).

Repurchase agreements (repos).

Treasury bills (already discussed in Chapter 6).

Commercial Paper

Commercial paper (CP) is an unsecured promise by the issuing company to pay the investor a certain number of dollars on a stated maturity date. If the proceeds are used to finance current transactions (that is, not added to capital) and mature in less than 270 days, the issuers are exempted from registering the issue as a security offering.

Commercial paper is a debt instrument that is offered sometimes as a "discount instrument" and sometimes as "principal plus interest." In the case of a discounted instrument, no interest payments are made. Instead, the price paid to buy the instrument is lower than the face value, which is paid to the buyer at maturity. The difference between the price paid and the face value is the interest earned on the investment. For a plus-interest instrument, the client pays the full face value to buy the paper and receives the face value plus the interest accrued at maturity.

Neither type of instrument has a fixed interest rate. Instead, the rate is negotiated at the time of purchase, and the interest is calculated from face or full value. To receive the interest, the buyer must, for all practical purposes, hold the instrument until maturity. If the paper is sold during its life, its price is subject to market fluctuations.

TRY THIS:

True or False? Commercial paper is a municipal short-term loan backed by the full faith and credit of the issuing city.

HERE'S WHY:

This statement is False. Commercial paper is a *corporate* short-term loan.

Most of the CP purchased by investors is held to maturity. Part of the reason for this is that on average, CP has a very short duration (less than 30 days). The other reason is that, while dealers and issuers usually buy back paper from investors who need to sell it to raise cash, the secondary market for CP is not nearly as well developed as it is for other money market instruments. Thus CP is not suitable for trading.

CP trades in pieces as small as $50,000 or as large as several $100 million. Recently, municipalities have begun to enter the CP market by selling short-term paper to investors who can benefit from the exemption from federal income taxes that this paper offers. Foreign companies have also begun tapping this relatively low-cost source of funds.

TRY THIS:

True or False? Plus-interest payment is when a client pays half the full face value to buy the paper and receives the face value plus the interest accrued at maturity.

HERE'S WHY:

This statement is False. Plus-interest payment is when the client pays the *full* face value and receives the face value plus interest accrued at maturity.

CP can be divided into two main classifications based on the type of issuer: direct issue paper and dealer paper.

Direct issues are sold directly by the issuing companies. These companies are so large, and they are in the commercial paper market so often, that it is cost-effective for them to build and maintain a dedicated in-house CP sales force. Direct placement takes place between a bank and its customers. Examples of direct issuers are the large finance companies and the largest public corporations. Smaller companies, on the other hand, use dealers to sell their CP when they are in the market. For this service they generally pay a fee to the dealer of approximately .125% of the offering proceeds. **Dealer-sold paper** is often purchased by the dealer in bulk and then sold to individual customers.

CP, regardless of the issuer, is always unsecured debt. It is backed only by the full faith and credit of the issuing corporation but not by a specific item against any of the issuer's assets or collateral. For this reason, investors need to pay close attention to the credit ratings of CP issues. CP is rated 1, 2, 3, or 4 by the major ratings services. Number 1 paper is the safest, and number 4 paper is either already in or well on its way to default. A typical CP rating is expressed as "A1-P2," meaning that Standard & Poor's rates it a "1" and Moody's rates it a 2.

Often a company with a low credit rating gets its bank to issue a letter of credit guaranteeing the paper or an insurance company to issue a financial guarantee bond covering it. This way, paper that would have been rated 3 can come to market with a 1. Even after paying the bank or insurance company a fee for providing the guarantee, the company's net cost of borrowing is often reduced by obtaining these third-party guarantees.

Transactions in commercial paper settle same day: if you buy today, you must pay today. Dealers must pay for commercial paper on the day of purchase. When dealers resell the paper to their customers, the new owners must pay on the day of purchase. Usually both transactions—from corporation to dealer and from dealer to customer—occur on the same day. Control and accuracy are therefore mandatory due to the large sums of money involved and the limited time for settling all the daily transactions.

The normal method of payment is by Fed funds. Because of the transaction size, most settlement is effected between banks through the use of the Fed wire, a communications network among member banks of the Federal Reserve System. Funds received through this vehicle do not follow the usual overnight or several-day fund clearance cycle experienced with checks. Because a recipient of Fed funds can use the money when received as if it were cash, Fed funds are considered same-day funds.

TRY THIS:

Transactions in commercial paper settle
a. Next day.
b. Same day.
c. Any day.
d. Every day.

HERE'S WHY:

The correct answer is (b). CP transactions settle the same day. The day you buy it is the day you have to pay for it.

Banker's Acceptances

Banker's acceptances (BAs) are bills of exchange that are issued and guaranteed by a bank for payment within one to six months. The funds raised through their sale provide manufacturers and exporters with operating capital between the time of production or exporting and the time of payment by purchasers. In effect, the bank "accepts" evidence of the value of goods being either manufactured or exported. For that evidence, it issues its "acceptance" in the form of a certificate, which can then be bought and sold as a security.

Suppose a U.S. importer wants to acquire goods from a foreign manufacturer. Because the goods must be produced and shipped, the foreign manufacturer wants to be assured of payment and does not want to wait until the goods are received in the United States. The importer goes to a U.S. bank with which it has a business relationship and applies for a letter of credit. The letter of credit is sent to a foreign bank representing the manufacturer. The letter, along with the merchandise invoice (that is, bill of exchange), is returned to the importer's bank, which stamps "Accepted" on the invoice. The importer's bank pays the foreign manufacturer through the foreign bank, and the banker's acceptance is thus created.

This procedure can be reversed. A foreign importer can apply to an overseas bank for a letter of credit and an American manufacturer can be paid before delivery is actually taken. The "paper" is therefore daily guaranteed by two parties: the accepting bank and the importing firm.

BAs can also be used by a domestic company to finance merchandise located in one foreign country and awaiting shipment to an importer in another foreign country.

TRY THIS:

True or False? Banks involved with international commerce may issue banker's acceptances for financing purposes.

HERE'S WHY:

This statement is True.

BAs are bearer instruments that are sold to investors as discounted instruments. Since the instrument is discounted, the difference between what investors pay for the BA and the face value they are paid at maturity is the interest earned.

Interest on BAs is computed based on a 360-day year. Computations are therefore made following the procedures used for U.S. Treasury bills. Trades in BAs settle the same day.

The issuing bank can keep the BA or sell it. If it keeps the certificate, it has a loan on its books, between it and the importer. Any loan has an effect on the banks' reserve requirements, which is the percentage of their money that, by law, it may not lend out. By selling the BA, however, it applies the sales proceeds—the investor's money—to the loan, thereby freeing up bank funds for other loans.

If the bank sells the loan, it endorses it, thereby guaranteeing it, and the loan becomes a banker's acceptance.

TRY THIS:

A short-term debt issued by banks and used in international trade is
a. Stock.
b. Bond.
c. Banker's acceptance.
d. Commercial paper.

HERE'S WHY:

The correct answer is (c). BAs are bills of exchange guaranteed (accepted) by a bank or trust company for payment within one to six months. They are used to provide manufacturers and exporters with capital to operate between the time of manufacturing (or exporting) and payment by purchasers.

LET'S TRY ANOTHER ONE:

True or False? A banker's acceptance is a mortgage issued and guaranteed by a bank for payment within six months.

HERE'S WHY:

This statement is False. A BA is a bill of exchange, not a mortgage. Just want to see if you're paying attention!

Certificates of Deposit

A **certificate of deposit** (CD) is a negotiable security issued by commercial banks against money deposited over a period of time. The value of CDs varies depending on the amount of deposit and maturity. The CD is one of the most popular investment vehicles in America—for several reasons:

1. *Various maturities* allow investors to select the term that best suits their needs and objectives. The shortest-term CDs mature just seven days after they are issued, although CDs with maturities of 30, 60, 90, 180, and 360 days are more popular with investors.
2. *Various forms* allow investors to select the one to best meet their needs and objectives. These forms include not only traditional fixed rate, fixed term CDs (that are bought and redeemed at par), but also zero-coupon CDs (that are bought at discount and par at maturity), and variable rate CDs (that are bought at par but pay an interest rate that is periodically adjusted to reflect changes in market rates).
3. *CDs' competitive returns* rival the returns offered by other secure, fully taxable, short-term investment vehicles.
4. *The credit risk is minimal* because deposits in a banking institution in one name are insured up to $100,000 by the Federal Deposit Insurance Corporation (FDIC) or by the Federal Savings and Loan Insurance Corporation (FSLIC).
5. *Liquidity* is a feature if the CD is issued by one of America's leading banks. Investors more interested in liquidity than in yield generally invest only in CDs issued by the top-tier money center banks. The reason is that the secondary market is fairly well developed. It is possible to buy and sell these instruments at almost any time at a fair price and with minimal transaction costs.

The price investors pay for this liquidity is a lower yield. Investors who are more yield-conscious generally hire a CD broker to place their CDs with banks and savings and loans offering the highest yield, regardless of where the banks and S&Ls are located. Because there is no secondary market for CDs issued by small banks and S&Ls, investors needing their funds prior to the CD's maturity date have to redeem them with the issuing institution and incur a six-month interest penalty.

TRY THIS:

True or False? Short-term debt instruments issued by banks are certificates of deposit.

HERE'S WHY:

This statement is True. The shortest term is 7 days, and the longest term (though not really short in comparison) is 360 days.

There are four types of CDs:

1. Domestic CDs are issued by American banks to investors in the United States.
2. Eurodollar CDs are issued by American banks to investors abroad.
3. Yankee CDs are issued to investors in the United States by U.S. branches of foreign banks.
4. Savings and loan institutions also issue CDs.

TRY THIS:

True or False? The interest on CDs is computed on a 365-day basis.

HERE'S WHY:

This statement is False. The interest on CDs is computed on a 360-day basis. The issue can be either plus interest or discounted as with commercial paper. Investors prefer the discounted form because the yield can be understood easily, as in the case of T-bills.

Repurchase Agreements

A **repurchase transaction** (**repo**) is the sale of a security from a seller to a buyer with the simultaneous agreement from the seller to re-purchase the security at a fixed price (or pricing rate) on a specified future date. Thus, while a repo is technically a "sale," functionally it represents a loan from the buyer to the seller with the security used as collateral.

The most common repurchase transaction is a U.S. government bond dealer selling U.S. government bonds to an investor and at the same time agreeing to repurchase the bonds the next day at a slightly higher price. The difference in price represents the return to investors. In this type of transaction the dealer is able to use the investor's money to finance its bond inventory at a lower cost than what a bank would charge to finance it. Investors, on the other hand, are able to lock in a fixed return on an overnight investment, generally at a higher rate than they could get from a money market fund.

Although most repos are overnight transactions, corporate investment officers frequently enter into longer-term repo transactions (up to a month or more) if the rate offered them by a dealer is particularly attractive, or if they expect interest rates to decline and wish to lock in a fixed rate. Further, the repo market is not limited to government securities. Repo transactions can also be done against certificates of deposit, banker's acceptances, high-quality corporate bonds, U.S. government agencies, mortgage securities, or other high-quality liquid securities.

High-quality liquid securities are needed because, in the event the seller is either unable or unwilling to repurchase the securities on the agreed-upon date and at the agreed-upon price, the buyer must then sell the securities in the open market to recoup the investment. Only high-quality, liquid securities offer repo investors real protection in this situation.

If the transaction is done properly, investors should not have any market risk. If, over the course of the transaction, the market value of the collateral should either rise or fall, the market gain or market loss accrues to the seller and not to the investor. The investor, by agreeing in advance to a specific repurchase price (or pricing rate), effectively locks in a return regardless of how changing market conditions affect the market value of the collateral.

TRY THIS:

In the case of a discounted instrument,
a. Dividends are paid.
b. Interest payments are made.
c. No interest payments are made.
d. Face value is increased.

HERE'S WHY:

The correct answer is (c). In a discounted instrument, no interest payments are made. Instead, the price paid to buy the instrument is lower than the face value, which is paid to the buyer at maturity. The difference between the price paid and the face value is the interest earned on the investment.

Treasury Bills

Probably the best-known money market instrument, **T-bills** are short-term discount obligations of the U.S. Treasury. They are popular investments for institutions because of their short maturities and ready marketability. The market for them is so large and efficient and Treasuries are so liquid that they are frequently said to be "cash equivalent." They are discussed in more detail in Chapter 6.

Municipal Notes

Municipal notes, as discussed in Chapter 5, have maturities of less than one year. State and local government use such short-term municipal borrowing to bridge gaps in financing. Municipalities usually issue notes at discounts from face value (like Treasury bills), with the interest paid at maturity. The types of notes frequently issued by state and local governments are tax anticipation notes, revenue anticipation notes, bond anticipation notes, general obligation notes, and project notes.

TRY THIS:

The market for dealers who trade riskless, short-term securities is the
a. Stock market.
b. Options market.
c. Government securities market.
d. Money market.

HERE'S WHY:

The correct answer is (d). Securities traded in the money market include T-bills, CDs, BAs, and commercial paper. The short-term debt (of less than one year to maturity) is usually issued at a discount and does not bear interest.

Call Loans

These are short-term loans that banks extend to securities dealers and brokers. These loans are considered safe because the brokerage firms put up securities as collateral. Their name derives from the fact that either the lender or the borrower can terminate them—that is, "call" them in—simply by giving one day's notice.

Federal Funds (Fed Funds)

Member banks of the Fed hold their required reserves as deposits with the district Federal Reserve Bank. On any given day, a bank may be over or under its reserve requirement. Since the Fed itself does not pay interest on the deposited reserve funds, banks with an excess of such funds can lend part or all of the excess to a bank that needs funds to reach its reserve requirement. Because of the supply/demand dynamics, a market has developed for these "federal funds."

The sale of Fed funds is called a "straight transaction," and it is made on a one-day, unsecured basis. The bank selling the funds instructs the Federal Reserve Bank to charge its account and credit the account of the buying (that is, the borrowing) bank. On the following day, the transaction is reversed. The exchange is made electronically through the Federal Reserve System's communication network, known as the "Fed wire." No physical delivery is made.

8

Accrued Interest, Quotations, and Basis Pricing

If a transaction involves bonds, interest has to be accrued and paid by the buyer to the seller. Corporate bonds, for example, pay interest at six-month intervals. Their representative banks or agents pay, to the bondholder, the full six months' interest at the time the interest is due. The owner who bought the bonds sometime during the six months between interest payments owes some of the interest to the seller, who owned the bonds for the first part of the period. This interest is said to have accrued to the owner; that is, it became due to the owner as the six months passed.

Keeping track of and collecting the accrued interest could be cumbersome for the seller of the bonds. So the buyer pays all the accrued interest due to the seller as of the day that the transaction settles. Then the new owner receives the full six months' payment when the interest is due and paid.

EXAMPLE:

XYZ 8% AO 2010 pays 8% interest, or $80 per $1,000 bond. Since the bond pays interest every April and October (AO), the six-month interest is $40 per $1,000 bond. Owner A holds the bond for three months after an interest payment date and then sells it. Owner B who acquires the bonds pays $20 (or half of the interest that would accrue in a six-month period) to the seller at the time of the transaction. Three months later, XYZ Corporation, the issuer, pays the new owner $40, representing a full six months of interest. The new owner has received $40 but paid $20 accrued interest to the seller at the time of purchase. The remaining $20 ($40 − $20 = $20) represents the interest accrued to the new owner for the second three months.

When computing interest on corporate and municipal bonds, you assume that the year contains 360 days and that each month contains 30 days. The month of sale is counted in actual days.

EXAMPLE:

If XYZ bonds are acquired on a settlement date of April 1 and sold on a settlement date of July 1, the owner receives all the interest accrued during the period.

April 1 to April 30	30 days
May 1 to May 31	30 days
June 1 to June 30	30 days
Total	90 days

The formula is

$$\text{Accrued interest} = \frac{\text{Principal}}{1} \times \frac{\text{Interest}}{100} \times \frac{\text{Number of days}}{\text{Base number}}$$

The face amount of the XYZ bond is $1,000. The interest rate is 8%, the number of days owned is 90. The base number of days is 360. So

$$\text{Accrued interest} = \frac{\$1,000}{1} \times \frac{8}{100} \times \frac{90 \text{ days}}{360 \text{ days}}$$

$$= \frac{\$1,000}{1} \times \frac{2}{25} \times \frac{1}{4}$$

$$= \frac{\$2,000}{100}$$

$$= \$20$$

Interest calculations for different types of debt instruments (bonds, notes, bills, CDs, and the like) call for different bases. Just insert the appropriate number of days into that portion of the formula and you can figure out that instrument's interest.

TRY THIS:

If an 8% bond pays $80 per year per $1,000 of face value, what will it pay semiannually?

HERE'S WHY:

Very simply, $40 per half year, since it pays $80 for a full year.

Interest continues to accrue to the bond's seller up to but not including settlement day, on which date the accrued interest is paid to the seller. Let's take a look at another example.

EXAMPLE:

On April 4, you purchase $1,000 XYZ 8% AO 2005 @ 96, which settles on April 11. Because the bond pays interest on April 1 and October 1 (AO), you owe the seller interest from April 1 through April 10. Counting the days from April 1, the first day of the interest period, up through but not including the settlement date of April 11, you get 10 days. You owe 10 days of interest. Let's calculate the accrued interest:

$$\text{Accrued interest} = \underset{1}{\overset{\overset{\text{(face amount)}}{\$1,000}}{}} \times \underset{100}{\overset{\overset{\text{(interest rate)}}{8}}{}} \times \underset{360}{\overset{\overset{\text{(days)}}{10}}{}} = \$2.23$$

You pay the seller $960 (.96 × $1,000 face value) plus the accrued interest of $2.23.

On August 29, you sell the bonds at a price of 96 for settlement on September 5.

Now let's see the calculations on the sale of the bond. From April 11 through September 4, you accrue interest. Counting from April 11 through but not including the settlement date of September 5, you get 144 days, during which interest has accrued to you. You are entitled to 144 days of accrued interest.

	Days
April	20
May	30
June	30
July	30
August	30
September	4
Total	144

$$\text{Accrued interest} = \frac{\$1,000}{1} \times \frac{8}{100} \times \frac{144}{360} = \$32.00$$

Because you paid $2.23 in accrued interest when you purchased the bond and you earned actual interest of $32, which equals the accrued interest for 144 days, the buyer of the bond must pay you a total of $34.23, which represents a total of 154 days.

On October 1, the corporation's agent pays $40 to the recorded holder of the bond. The purchaser of your bond has accumulated 26 days of accrued interest, for a sum of $5.77. The new owner, having paid you $34.23, ends up with the $5.77 difference.

Note that the corporation authorizes its agent to pay the entire six-month interest payment to the recorded holder. The parties who buy or sell bonds during the period simply settle the accrued interest among themselves.

EXAMPLE:

First customer:	Receives accrued interest at time of sale	$ 2.23
You:	Pay at time of purchase	$ 2.23
	Receive at time of sale	34.23
	Accrues to you	32.00
Third customer:	Pays to you at time of purchase	$34.23
	Receives from corporation	40.00
	Accrues to the new owner	5.77
Total		$40.00
Total paid by company		$40.00

TRY THIS:

Wynn Doe purchases a corporate bond $1,000 RAM 9% JJ (January 1 and July 1) 2006 at 93. The trade date is April 9, and the settlement date is April 16. For how many days of accrued interest should be accounted?
a. 105.
b. 106.
c. 16.
d. 15.

HERE'S WHY:

The correct answer is (a). The last interest payment was given on January 1. W. Doe bought on April 9, but settled on April 16. Count the number of days from January 1 to April 15 (assume 30 days/month). Accrued interest is calculated up to but not including settlement day.

Jan., Feb., Mar.,   +   Apr.
90   15   = 105

LET'S TRY ANOTHER ONE:

Accrued interest on municipal bonds is computed up to and including
a. Trade date.
b. Trade date plus one.
c. Day prior to settlement date.
d. Settlement date.

HERE'S WHY:

The correct answer is (c). The computation is exactly the same as for
corporate bonds. Interest continues to accrue to the bond's seller up to
but not including settlement day, on which date the accrued interest is
paid to the seller.

Governments trade on an actual/actual basis, a 365- or 366-day
year. Accrued interest is figured up to, but not including, settlement

TABLE 8–1.   **Number of days for Calculation of Accrued Interest.**

	Corporates and Municipals 360-Day Year	Governments 365-Day Year	366-Day Year
January	30	31	31
February	30	28	29
March	30	31	31
April	30	30	30
May	30	31	31
June	30	30	30
July	30	31	31
August	30	31	31
September	30	30	30
October	30	31	31
November	30	30	30
December	30	31	31
Total	360	365	366

date, just like corporates and municipals. However, because governments usually settle the next day, instead of five business days for corporates and municipals, coincidentally accrued interest on governments is figured to trade date.

The only other confusing ingredient in using actual days is that you must calculate the actual days divided by the actual days in the semiannual period, not the year. That also means you must divide the annual interest by two.

EXAMPLE:

Suppose you sell a U.S. Treasury 9% due February 15, 1994 on September 1 for settlement September 2. How much is the accrued interest?

	Number of Days	Number of days in Semiannual Period
August 15–31	17	17
September 1	1	30
	18	
October		31
November		30
December		31
January		31
February (to the 15th)		14
		184

$$\frac{\text{Accrued}}{\text{interest}} = \text{Principal} \times \frac{\text{Semiannual interest rate (half the annual rate)}}{} \times \frac{\text{Number of days of accrual}}{\text{Number of days in semiannual period}}$$

$$= \$1{,}000 \times \frac{.09}{.2} \times \frac{18}{184} = \frac{\$1{,}620}{368}$$

$$= \$4.40$$

Bond Quotations

The prices of bonds fluctuate in the marketplace just as stock prices do. Yet unlike stock quotations, bond quotations must contain specific details regarding not only the issuer, but also the rate of interest, maturity, and price. A quote like "Am Mot 6s '88 at 87" contains all the necessary details in concise form to notate the following:

Issuer "Am Mot" is American Motors.

Interest Rate "6s" is the notation for 6% interest. In other words, this bond pays 6% annual interest per bond. In dollars, this rate comes to $60 ($1,000 par × .06).

Maturity "'88" signifies that the bond matures in 1988. At this time, the par value is returned to whoever then holds the bond.

Price "at 87" indicates that this bond is trading at a price of 87, which translates into $870. If the bond were trading at par, the price would be "100" ($1,000). This Am Mot bond is said to be trading at a discount because its price is below par. If it were trading above 100, it would be trading at a premium.

As another example, the "AT&T 8.7s '02 at 107¼" signifies the 8.7% American Telephone and Telegraph bonds that pay $87 annual interest per bond, that mature in 2002, and that have a market price per bond of $1,072.50.

Price Notation

Bond prices can be quoted as a percentage of yield or as a percentage of the par or face value.

As a Percentage of Par

This is probably the simplest form of quote. To get the dollar value, simply add zero to the quoted price for each $1,000 of face value. For example,

97 becomes $970.

83 becomes $830.

107 becomes $1,070.

110 becomes $1,100.

Percentages are also used to convert other values to dollar figures. Corporate and U.S. bonds are priced at a percentage of face value, so that a quote of, say, "75" means "75%" of any par value. To get the dollar figure, simply multiply the decimal form of the percentage by the face amount. In this case, since "75" would mean "75%," or as a decimal, 0.75, you see that it reflects a price of $750 when multiplied by a par of $1,000. Obviously, as long as the par is $1,000, you can skip the decimal step. If it were the price of a $10,000 bond, it would be $10,000 × .75 or $7,500; for a $40,000 bond, $40,000 × .75, or $30,000.

EXAMPLES:

Quote	Percentage	Dollars
75	75%	$ 750
102	102	1,020
104½	104½	1,045

Fractions

The use of fractions presents only a minor difficulty in converting quotes to dollar values. You simply follow the same steps as for whole numbers or percentages, but you use the decimal forms of the fractions. (Note that, although "eighths" represent portions of $1 in stock prices, they represent portions of $10 in bond prices.)

EXAMPLE:

A quote of "91⅛" must be translated into decimal form before the standard conversion can be carried out:

Percent	Decimal	Dollars
$91\frac{1}{8}$	.91125	$911.25
$83\frac{1}{2}$	.8350	835.00

To make these conversions quickly in your head, it would help to memorize the values in Table 8-2.

Some bonds, particularly U.S. government securities, have such good marketability in a keenly competitive market that they trade in thirty-seconds or even sixty-fourths rather than eighths. To obtain the dollar values, you follow the same steps, but you use Table 8-3 to convert the fractions into decimals. (This table assumes par to be $1,000.) In this table, each thirty-second or sixty-fourth is accompanied by the appropriate dollar value—again some portion of $10. The plus signs in the "32nds" columns have a special significance. If a thirty-second has a plus sign after it, then it is the equivalent of the next highest sixty-fourth. For example, a $^{10}/_{32}+$ is the same value as $^{21}/_{64}$ $(^{10}/_{32} + ^{1}/_{64} = {}^{20}/_{64} + ^{1}/_{64})$.

Government bond quotes look like this:

(a) 96.6   (b) 98.8+

The numbers to the right of the decimals represent thirty-seconds. Price (a) is therefore $96^{6}/_{32}$, which translates to $96^{3}/_{16}$ or $961.875. Price (b) is $98^{8}/_{32}$ plus $^{1}/_{64}$, which comes to $98^{17}/_{64}$ or $982.65625. You will also see 96.06 or 98.08+; it means the same thing.

TABLE 8-2   Decimal values of increments
of one-eighth.

$\frac{1}{8}$ = 0.125 or $1.25 per bond
$\frac{1}{4}$ = 0.250 or $2.50 per bond
$\frac{3}{8}$ = 0.375 or $3.75 per bond
$\frac{1}{2}$ = 0.500 or $5.00 per bond
$\frac{5}{8}$ = 0.625 or $6.25 per bond
$\frac{3}{4}$ = 0.750 or $7.50 per bond
$\frac{7}{8}$ = 0.875 or $8.75 per bond

TABLE 8-3. Dollar Equivalents of Thirty-seconds and Sixty-fourths per $1,000 of Face Value.

32nds	64ths	Per $1,000	32nds	64ths	Per $1,000
+	1	.15625	16+	33	5.15625
1	2	.31250	17	34	5.31250
1+	3	.46875	17+	35	5.46875
2	4	.62500	18	36	5.62500
2+	5	.78125	18+	37	5.78125
3	6	.93750	19	38	5.93750
3+	7	1.09375	19+	39	6.09375
4	8	1.25000	20	40	6.25000
4+	9	1.40625	20+	41	6.40625
5	10	1.56250	21	42	6.56250
5+	11	1.71875	21+	43	6.71875
6	12	1.87500	22	44	6.87500
6+	13	2.03125	22+	45	7.03125
7	14	2.18750	23	46	7.18750
7+	15	2.34375	23+	47	7.34375
8	16	2.50000	24	48	7.50000
8+	17	2.65625	24+	49	7.65625
9	18	2.81250	25	50	7.81250
9+	19	2.96875	25+	51	7.96875
10	20	3.12500	26	52	8.12500
10+	21	3.28125	26+	53	8.28125
11	22	3.43750	27	54	8.43750
11+	23	3.59375	27+	55	8.59375
12	24	3.75000	28	56	8.75000
12+	25	3.90625	28+	57	8.90625
13	26	4.06250	29	58	9.06250
13+	27	4.21875	29+	59	9.21875
14	28	4.37500	30	60	9.37500
14+	29	4.53125	30+	61	9.53125
15	30	4.68750	31	62	9.68750
15+	31	4.84375	31+	63	9.84375
16	32	5.00000	32	64	10.00000

The spread between a dealer's bid price (the price at which a dealer will buy a bond) and ask price (the price at which a dealer will sell it) is often just a thirty-second of a point. For example, a dealer might bid a bond at 94.05 and offer it at 94.06. That is just a little over 31 cents per bond.

TRY THIS:

A quotation of 84.8 means dollar value of
a. $84.80.
b. $840.80.
c. $842.50.
d. $848.00.

HERE'S WHY:

The correct answer is (b).

Basis Points

The term "point" means different things in stocks and bonds. As we mentioned earlier, a point in stock quotations is the same as $1. However, in bond quotation, a point is $10. For instance, if a bond's price changed from, say, 80 to 81, it is said to have changed by 1 point, that is, from $800 to $810 dollars.

A point should not be confused with a basis point, which in bond quotes is one-hundredth of a percentage point (.01%). For instance, if a Treasury bill's price drops from, say, "7.17 basis" to "7.10 basis," it is said to have declined seven basis points.

TRY THIS:

A basis point is
a. 10%.
b. 1%.
c. 0.1%.
d. 0.01%.

> **HERE'S WHY:**
>
> The correct answer is (d). In bond quotations a basis point is one-hundredth of a percentage point.

Basis Pricing

Some municipal and government securities trade at a "basis." To understand this concept of basis pricing, you must understand yields, which is the percentage of return on investment. Even though we discussed yield in Chapter 3, a review may be helpful. In the bond market, there are three types of yield:

1. Nominal yield.
2. Current yield.
3. Yield to maturity.

Nominal Yield

The percentage of interest paid on the face value of the instrument.

EXAMPLE:

A $1,000 bond with an interest obligation of 7% has a nominal yield of 7% (.07 × $1,000). It pays $70 interest per year on each $1,000 bond.

Current Yield

Bonds pay interest based on the face value. The interest or coupon rate remains the same regardless of fluctuations in the market price of the bond. The investor is concerned with the return or the amount of interest received on the amount of money paid. Current yield tells the investor what that return is, given the price of the bond.

EXAMPLE:

The bond in our previous example is selling for 120; that is, the bond costs you $1,200 to acquire. It still pays only $70 in interest (7% on the face value of $1,000). Although, as the bond's owner, you receive $70, the return is based on a cost of $1,200. Your current yield is therefore only 5.83% ($70 divided by $1,200).

Yield to Maturity

This type of yield takes into account the net dollar amount that an investor can expect if the bond is held to its maturity date.

EXAMPLE:

A $1,000 bond paying 7% interest will mature in 30 years. When you purchase it for $1,200, the bond has 20 years of life left. At the end of 20 years (at maturity), the corporation is obligated to retire the debt for $1,000 (face value). If you paid $1,200 today for the bond, you will receive only $1,000 at maturity. It appears that you will lose $200.

But, maybe not. Divide the $200 loss (or amortize it) over the 20 years remaining: $200 ÷ 20 years = $10 per year. You are losing $10 per year, which accumulates on this transaction. Yet the bond is going to pay you $70 per year in interest. So over 20 years, you actually earned an average $60 per year for every year you own the bond. In dollars, this is your yield to maturity.

Basis Price

Converting certain securities to and from their dollar prices to their yields to maturity or basis prices during the course of a busy trading day would be very cumbersome. Therefore, certain securities are traded on their yields to maturity, known as basis prices.

EXAMPLE:

A $1,000 bond with a 6% coupon, selling at 5.50 basis, costs more than $1,000. Conversely, a $1,000 bond with a 6% coupon, selling at a 6.50 basis, trades for less than $1,000.

The computation of yield to maturity or base price is complex. But a "rule-of-thumb" formula gives you an approximate figure. The formula is

$$\text{Yield to maturity} = \frac{\text{Annual interest amount} \pm \text{Amortized premium or discount}}{(\text{Face amount} + \text{current value})/2}$$

EXAMPLE:

Investor Watson purchases a $1,000 Russel County KY FA 8% 2011 @ 95 on trade date January 21, 1986. The bond matures in 25 years (2011 – 1986). The price of 95 translates into $950. At maturity, the bondholder receives $1,000 or $50 in capital gains ($1,000 – $950). You must amortize the $50 discount. $50 ÷ 25 years = $2 annual amortization. The 8% bond would pay $80 in interest payment per year. Therefore,

$$\text{Yield to maturity} = \frac{\$80 + \$2}{(\$1,000 + \$950)/2} = \frac{\$82}{\$975} = .841 = 8.41\%$$

The "rule-of-thumb" formula gives you the yield to maturity of 8.41%. Or you could say that the bond was purchased at a "8.41 basis."

TRY THIS:

True or False? Another term for basis price, as used in municipal securities and other debt instruments, is yield to maturity.

HERE'S WHY:

This statement is True.

Bid and Offer System

The quotes for dollar-priced securities contain a bid (purchase) price and an offer (sale) price. On this type of quote, the bid is lower than the offer.

EXAMPLE:

A ZAP bond is a debt of ZAP Corporation with a 6% coupon expiring in 1995. It is referred to as "ZAP 6% FA 95." The basis quote is 6.50–5.50. The "6.50" means that the highest price anyone will pay for the bond will yield 6.50% to maturity. The lowest price at which anyone will offer the bonds for sale will yield the new owner 5.50%. If you sell the bond at the bid (6.50), you actually receive less than $1,000. If you buy at the offer (5.50), you would pay more than $1,000. Either way, the bond yields only 6% on $1,000.

Basis quotes confuse some people because the bid appears to be higher than the offer. But remember, the lower the yield, the higher the price: the higher the yield, the lower the price.

TRY THIS:

True or False? The rule in basis pricing is the higher the price, the higher the yield.

HERE'S WHY:

This statement is False. It's the *lower* the price, the higher the yield.

Glossary

Accrued Interest   (1) The amount of interest due the seller, from the buyer, upon settlement of a bond trade. (2) Prorated interest due since the last interest payment date.

Active Bonds (The "Free Crowd")   A category of debt securities that the NYSE Floor Department expects to trade frequently and that are consequently handled freely in the trading ring in much the same manner as stocks. See *Inactive Bonds.*

Active Box   A physical location where securities are held awaiting action on them.

Adjustment Bonds   See *Income (Adjustment) Bonds.*

Aftermarket   A market for a security either over-the-counter or on an exchange after an initial public offering has been made. See *Hot Issue; Stabilization; Withholding.*

Agreement Among Underwriters   An agreement among members of an underwriting syndicate specifying the syndicate manager, his or her duties, and his or her privileges, among other things. See *Underwriter's Retention; Underwriting Agreement.*

All-or-None (AON) Offering   A "best-efforts" offering of newly issued securities in which the corporation instructs the investment banker to cancel the entire offering (sold and unsold) if all of it cannot be distributed.

All-or-None Order   An order to buy or sell more than one round lot of stock at one time and at a designated price or better. It must not be executed until both conditions can be satisfied simultaneously.

"And Interest"   A bond transaction in which the buyer pays the seller a contract price plus interest accrued since the corporation's last interest payment.

AON Offering   See *All-or-None (AON) Offering.*

AON Order   See *All-or-None (AON) Order.*

Arbitrage   The simultaneous purchase and sale of the same or equal securities in such a way as to take advantage of price differences prevailing in separate markets. See *Bona Fide Arbitrage; Risk Arbitrage.*

Arbitrage Bonds   All bonds found in violation of federal arbitrage regulations as deemed by the Internal Revenue Service. If the IRS deems a bond an arbitrage bond, then the interest becomes taxable and must therefore be included in each bondholder's gross income for federal tax purposes.

Arbitrageur   One who engages in arbitrage.

As Agent   The role of a broker/dealer firm when it acts as an intermediary, or broker, between its customer and another customer, a market maker, or a contrabroker. For this service, the firm receives a stated commission or fee. This is an "agency transaction." See *As Principal.*

As Principal   The role of a broker/dealer firm when it buys and sells for its own account. In a typical transaction, it buys from a market maker or contrabroker and sells to a customer at a fair and reasonable markup; if it buys from a customer and sells to the market maker at a higher price, the trade is called a markdown. See *As Agent.*

Ask-Bid System   A system used to place a market order. A market order is one the investor wants executed immediately at the best prevailing price. The market order to buy requires a purchase at the lowest offering (asked) price, and a market order to sell requires a sale at the highest (bid) price. The bid price is what the dealer is willing to pay for the stock, while the ask price is the price at which the dealer will sell to individual investors. The difference between the bid and ask prices is the spread. See *Bid-and-asked Quotations.*

At-the-Close Order   An order to be executed, at the market, at the close, or as near as practicable to the close of trading for the day .

At-the-Market   (1) A price representing what a buyer would pay and what a seller would take in an arm's-length transaction assuming normal competitive forces; (2) an order to buy or sell immediately at the currently available price.

At-the-Money   A term used to describe a security option where the strike price and market price are the same.

At-the-Opening (Opening Only) Order   An order to buy or sell at a limited price on the initial transaction of the day for a given security; if unsuccessful, it is automatically canceled.

Auction Marketplace   A term used to describe an organized exchange where transactions are held in the open and any exchange member present may join in.

Away from Me   When a market maker does not initiate a quotation, transaction, or market in an issue, he or she says it is "away from me."

Away from the Market   An order where the limit bid is below (or the limit offer is above) the quote for the security. For example, if a quote for a security is 20 to 20½, a limit order to buy at 19 is away from the market.

Baby Bond   A bond with a face value of less than $1,000, usually in $100 denominations.

Backing Away   The practice of an OTC market maker who refuses to honor his or her quoted bid-and-asked prices for at least 100 shares, or 10 bonds, as the case may be. This action is outlawed under the NASD Rules of Fair Practice.

Back Office   An industry expression used to describe nonsales departments of a brokerage concern, particularly a firm's P&S and cashier departments.

Balance Orders   The pairing off of each issue traded in the course of a day by the same member to arrive at a net balance of securities to receive or deliver. The net difference between buyers and sellers on the opening of the market allows the specialist to open the market appropriately.

Balloon Effect   A term used to describe a serial bond issue having lower principal repayments in the early years of its life and higher principal repayments in the later years.

BAN   See *Bond Anticipation Note.*

Bank Dealer   A bank engaged in buying and selling government securities, municipal securities, or certain money market instruments.

Banker's Acceptances   Bills of exchange guaranteed (accepted) by a bank or trust company for payment within one to six months. Used to provide manufacturers and exporters with capital to operate between the time of manufacturing (or exporting) and payment by purchasers. Bids and offers in the secondary marketplace are at prices discounted from the face value.

Banks for Cooperatives (Co-op)   An agency under the supervision of the Farm Credit Administration that makes and services loans for farmers' cooperative financing. The agency is capitalized by the issuance of bonds whose interest is free from state and local income taxes.

Basis Point   One one-hundredth of a percentage point. For example, if a Treasury bill yielding 7.17% changes in price so that it now yields 7.10%, it is said to have declined seven basis points.

Basis Price Odd-Lot Order   An odd-lot order executed on a fictitious round-lot price somewhere between the prevailing bid and offering, if (1) the issue doesn't trade throughout the day, (2) the spread is at least two full points, and (3) the customer requests such an execution.

Bearer Bond   A bond that does not have the owner's name registered on the books of the issuing corporation and that is payable to the bearer.

Bearer Form   Securities issued in such a form as not to allow for the owner's name to be imprinted on the security. The bearer of the security is presumed to be the owner who collects interest by clipping and depositing coupons semiannually.

Beneficial Owner   The owner of securities who receives all the benefits, even though they are registered in the street name of a brokerage firm or nominee name of a bank handling his or her account.

Best-Efforts Offering   An offering of newly issued securities in which the investment banker acts merely as an agent of the corporation, promising only his best efforts in making the issue a success but not guaranteeing the corporation its money for any unsold portion. See *All-or-None Offering.*

Bid-and-Asked Quotation (or Quote)   The bid is the highest price anyone has declared that he or she wants to pay for a security at a given time; the asked is the lowest price anyone will accept at the same time. See *Offer.*

Bidding Syndicate   Two or more underwriters working together to submit a proposal to underwrite a new issue of municipal securities. See *Syndicate*.

Blowout   A securities offering that sells out almost immediately.

Blue Sky Laws   State securities laws pertaining to registration requirements and procedures for issuers, broker/dealers, their employees, and other associated persons of those entities.

Blue Skying the Issue   The efforts of the underwriters' lawyers to analyze and investigate state laws regulating the distribution of securities and to qualify particular issues under these laws.

Board of Governors   (1) The governing body of the NASD, most of whom are elected by the general membership; the remainder are elected by the board itself. (2) See Federal Reserve Board.

Bona Fide Arbitrage   Arbitrage transactions by professional traders that take profitable advantage of prices for the same or convertible securities in different markets. The risk is usually minimal and the profit correspondingly small. See *Risk Arbitrage*.

Bond   A certificate representing creditorship in a corporation and issued by the corporation to raise capital. The company pays interest on a bond issue at specified dates and eventually redeems it at maturity, paying principal plus interest due. See *Bearer Bond; Collateral Trust Bond; Equipment Trust Bond; Income Bond; Mortgage Bond; Receiver's Certificate; Registered Bond; Serial Bond; Tax-Exempt Securities; U.S. Government Securities.*

Bond Amortization Fund   An account in a sinking fund. The issuer makes periodic deposits of money eventually to be used to purchase bonds on the open market or to pay the cost of calling bonds.

Bond and Preferred Stock Companies   Investment companies that emphasize stability of income. In the case of the municipal bond companies, income exempt from federal taxation is the chief goal.

Bond Anticipation Note (BAN)   A short-term municipal debt instrument usually offered on a discount basis. The proceeds of a forthcoming bond issue are pledged to pay the note at maturity.

Bond Broker   A member of the NYSE or any other exchange who executes orders in the bond room as a continuing practice.

Bonded Debt   The portion of an issuer's total indebtedness represented by outstanding bonds of various types.

Bond Fund   An investment company with a diversified portfolio of municipal securities. Units or shares in the investment company are sold to investors. Unit investment trusts (UITs) and managed funds are the two basic types of bond funds.

Bond Interest Distribution   Bonds that are traded at a market price and interest require an adjustment for the interest on the settlement date. The buyer therefore pays the seller the price plus interest accrued since the last payment date, and the buyer is thereby entitled to the next full payment of interest. The interest due is calculated by multiplying principal × rate × time. See *Ex-Dividend Date*.

Bond Issue   Bonds (1) sold in one or more series, (2) authorized under the same indenture or resolution, and (3) having the same date.

Bond Purchase Agreement   The contract between the issuer and underwriter that sets down the final terms, conditions, and prices by which the underwriter purchases an issue of municipal securities.

Bond Room   Formerly, the room at the New York Stock Exchange where bonds are traded.

Bought Deal   A commitment by a group of underwriters to guarantee performance by buying the securities from the issuer themselves, usually entailing some financial risk for the underwriters (or syndicate).

Box   A section of a cashier department where securities are stored temporarily. The department's responsibilities are sometimes subdivided to monitor both an active box and a free box for securities held by the firm.

Broker   An agent, often a member of a stock exchange firm or the head of a member firm, who handles the public's orders to buy and sell securities and commodities, for which service a commission is charged. The definition does not include a bank. See *Agent; As Principal*.

Broker's Broker   Also known as a municipal securities broker's broker, a person who deals only with other municipal securities brokers and dealers, not with the general public.

BW   An abbreviation for "Bid Wanted," indicating that the broker/dealer is soliciting buyers of the stock or bond.

Cabinet Crowd   See *Inactive Bonds*.

Cage, The   A slang expression used to describe a location where a brokerage firm's cashier department responsibilities are satisfied.

Call Feature (1) A feature of preferred stock through which it may be retired at the corporation's option by paying a price equal to or slightly higher than either the par or market value. (2) A bond feature by which all or part of an issue may be redeemed by the corporation before maturity and under certain specified conditions.

Call Protection A term used to describe a bond or preferred stock without a call feature or with a call feature that cannot be activated for a period of time.

Callable See *Call Feature.*

Can Crowd See *Inactive Bonds.*

Cash Contract A securities contract by which delivery of the certificates is due at the purchaser's office the same day as the date of the trade. See *Regular Way Contract; When Issued/When Distributed Contract.*

Cash on Delivery (COD) See *Delivery Versus Payment.*

Cash Trade A transaction involving specific securities, in which the settlement date is the same as the trade date.

Cashier Department A department of a broker/dealer organization responsible for the physical handling of securities and money, delivery and receipt, collateral loans, borrowing, lending, and transfer of securities, and other financial transactions.

Catastrophe (Calamity) Call An issuer's call for redemption of a bond issue when certain events occur, such as an accident at a construction site that severely affects the completion of the project.

CATS (Certificates of Accrual on Treasury Securities) Issues from the U.S. Treasury sold at a deep discount from their face value. They are called a zero-coupon securities because they require no interest payments during their lifetime, but they return the full face value at maturity. They cannot be called away. See *Zero-coupon Discount Security.*

CD See *Certificate of Deposit (CD).*

Central Bank (1) A Federal Reserve Bank situated in 1 of 12 banking districts in the United States. (2) The Federal Reserve System.

Central Certificate Service (CCS) Former name of the Depository Trust Company.

Certificate The actual piece of paper that is evidence of ownership or creditorship in a corporation. Water-marked certificates are finely engraved with delicate etchings to discourage forgery.

Certificates of Accrual on Treasury Securities   See *CATS*.

Certificate of Deposit (CD)   A negotiable money market instrument issued by commercial banks against money deposited with them for a specified period of time. CDs vary in size according to the amount of the deposit and the maturity period, and they may be redeemed before maturity only by sale in a secondary market.

Certificate of Incorporation   A state-validated certificate recognizing a business organization as a legal corporate entity. See *Charter*.

Certificate of Indebtedness (CI)   A federal bearer debt instrument in denominations of $1,000 to $500 million at a fixed interest rate, with maturities up to one year; they are fully marketable at a price reflecting their average rate of return.

Certified Security   A security whose ownership may be represented by a physical document. Also known as being available in "definitive form."

Charter   A document written by the founders of a corporation and filed with a state. The state approves the articles and then issues a certificate of incorporation. Together, the two documents become the charter and the corporation is recognized as a legal entity. The charter includes such information as the corporation's name, purpose, amount of shares, and the identity of the directors. Internal management rules are written by the founders in the bylaws. See *Certificate of Incorporation*.

Churning   A registered representative's improper handling of a customer's account: he or she buys and sells securities for a customer while intent only on the amount of commissions generated, ignoring the customer's interests and objectives.

Clean Opinion   See *Qualified Legal Opinion*.

Clearance   (1) The delivery of securities and monies in completion of a trade. (2) The comparison and/or netting of trades prior to settlement.

Clearinghouse Funds   (1) Money represented by a person's demand deposit account at a commercial bank. Withdrawals are accomplished by means of a check, which notifies the bank to transfer a sum to someone else's account, or to another bank. (2) Funds used in settlement of equity, corporate bond, and municipal bond settlement transactions. (3) A term used to mean next-day availability of funds. See *Federal Funds*.

Close   The final transaction price for an issue on the stock exchange at the end of a trading day.

Close-out Procedure The procedure taken by either party to a transaction when the contrabroker defaults; the disappointed purchaser may "buy in," and the rejected seller may "sell out" or liquidate.

Closing A meeting of all concerned parties on the date of delivery of a new issue of municipal securities, usually including the representatives of the issuer, bond counsel, and the purchasers or underwriters. The issuer makes physical delivery of the signed securities, and the required legal documents are exchanged.

Closing Quotation A market maker's final bid-and-asked prices for an issue as he or she ceases trading activities at the end of the business day.

Closing the Underwriting Contract The finalizing of contractual terms between an issuing corporation and the underwriters. Usually one week after the effective date, the certificates are given over to the underwriters and payment in full is made to the corporation.

COD Trade Cash on delivery. A general term to describe a transaction in which a seller is obliged to deliver securities to the purchaser or the purchaser's agent to collect payment.

COD Transaction A purchase of securities in behalf of a customer promising full payment immediately upon delivery of the certificates to an agent bank or broker/dealer.

Collateral Securities and other property pledged by a borrower to secure repayment of a loan.

Collateral Trust Bond A bond issue that is protected by a portfolio of securities held in trust by a commercial bank. The bond usually requires immediate redemption if the market value of the securities drops below or close to the value of the issue.

Commercial Paper Unsecured, short-term (usually a maximum of nine months) bearer obligations in denominations from $100,000 to $1 million, issued principally by industrial corporations, finance companies, and commercial factors at a discount from face value.

Commission A broker's fee for handling transactions for a client in an agency capacity.

Comparison A confirmation of a contractual agreement citing terms and conditions of a transaction between broker/dealers. This document must be exchanged by the contrafirms shortly after the trade date. See *Confirmation*.

Competitive Bidding A sealed envelope bidding process employed by various underwriter groups interested in handling the distribution of a securities issue. The contract is awarded to one group by the issuer on the basis of the highest price paid, interest rate expense, and tax considerations.

Concession   (1) In a municipal bond offering, the underwriters may offer a dollar discount from the offering price to MSRB members who are not taking part in the underwriting but who buy for their own or customers' accounts. (2) In a corporate underwriting, the underwriters may extend a dollar remuneration for each share or bond to selling group members who market the securities successfully.

Confirmation   An announcement of transaction terms and conditions and other pertinent information that is prepared for customer trade activities. It serves as a bill for customer purchases and as an advisory notice for sales.

Consumer Credit   Credit extended to the ultimate users of goods and services.

Contrabroker   A term used to describe the broker with whom a trade was made.

Conversion   A bond feature by which the owner may exchange his or her bonds for a specified number of shares of stock. Interest paid on such bonds is lower than the usual interest rate for straight debt issued. See *Conversion Parity; Conversion Price; Conversion Ratio.*

Conversion Arbitrage   A transaction where the arbitrageur buys the underlying security, but then buys a put and sells a call, both of which options have the same terms. See *Reversal Arbitrage.*

Conversion Parity   The equal dollar relationship between a convertible security and the underlying stock trading at or above the conversion price.

Conversion Price (Value)   In the case of convertible bonds, the price of the underlying common stock at which conversion can be made. The price is set by the issuing corporation and is printed in the indenture.

Conversion Ratio   The ratio indicating how many underlying shares may be obtained upon exchange of each convertible security. See *Convertible Security.*

Convertible Bond   Bond that can be exchanged for a specified number of another security, usually shares, at a prestated price. Convertibility typically enhances the bond's marketability.

Convertible (Security)   Any security that can be converted into another security. For example, a convertible bond or convertible preferred stock may be converted into the underlying stock of the same corporation at a fixed rate. The rate at which the shares of the bond or preferred stock are converted into the common is called the conversion ratio.

Cooling-off Period   See *Twenty-Day (Cooling-off) Period.*

Co-op   See *Banks for Cooperatives.*

Corporation   A business organization chartered by a state secretary as a recognized legal institution of and by itself and operated by an association of individuals, with the purpose of ensuring perpetuity and limited financial liability. See *Certificate of Incorporation; Charter.*

Coupon Bond   A bond with interest coupons attached. The coupons are clipped as they come due and are presented by the holders to their banks for payment. See *Bearer Bond; Registered Bond.*

Coupon Yield   See *Nominal Yield.*

Currency in Circulation   Paper bills and coins used by the general public to pay for goods and services.

Current Yield   The annual dollar interest paid by a bond dividend by its market price. It is the actual return rate, not the coupon rate. Example: Any bond carrying a 6% coupon and trading at 95 is said to offer a current yield of 6.3% ($60 coupon − $950 market price = 6.3%). Also sometimes referred to as current yield to maturity. See *Nominal Yield.*

Cushion Bond   A higher-than-current coupon debt instrument with a deferred call provision in its indenture offering a better current return and minimal price volatility (as compared with a bond without call protection). It normally trades with large premiums.

Dated Date   With regard to bonds and other debt instruments, the date from which interest is determined to accrue, upon the sale of the security. The buyer pays the amount equal to the interest accrued from the dated date to the settlement date and is reimbursed with the first interest payment on the security.

Day Order   A transaction order that remains valid only for the remainder of the trading on which it is entered.

Day Trading   The act of buying and selling a position during the same day.

Dealer   An individual or firm in the securities business acting as a principal rather than as an agent. See *As Agent; As Principal.*

Dealer Bank (1) A commercial bank's offering of a market in government or agency securities. (2) A bank department registered as a municipal securities dealer with the MSRB.

Dealer Book A publication by *The Bond Buyer* issued semiannually listing municipal bond dealers, municipal finance consultants, and bond attorneys within the United States. The book is colloquially referred to as the "Red Book" (the color of its cover), but it is really entitled *Directory of Municipal Bond Dealers of the United States*. Standard & Poor's Corporation prints a similar bond entitled *Securities Dealers of North America,* which includes Canadian dealers.

Debenture An unsecured debt offering by a corporation, promising only the general assets as protection for creditors. Sometimes the so-called "general assets" are only goodwill and reputation.

Debt Instrument The document specifying the terms and conditions of a loan between a lender and a borrower.

Debt Security Any security reflecting the loan of money that must be paid back to the lender in the future, such as a bill, note, or bond.

Deep Discount Bond A bond, although issued at par, that is currently selling below 80% of its par value. Not a bond sold at an original issue discount. See *Discount.*

Default The failure of a corporation to pay principal and/or interest on outstanding bonds or dividends on its preferred stock.

Defeasance (1) The substitution of a new debt for old debt. Specifically, a corporation replaces old, low-rate debt with securities having less face value but paying a higher interest. (2) A company could also have a broker/dealer buy up its bonds and convert them to a new issue of the company's stock, which is of equal value to the bonds. The broker can later sell the stock for a profit.

Delivery Versus Payment The purchase of securities in a cash account with instructions that payment will be made immediately upon the delivery of the securities, sometimes to the contra-broker but usually to an agent bank. Also known as "deliver against cash" (DAC). See *COD Trade.*

Demand Deposit A loan or checking account that gives its owner the right to withdraw funds from a commercial bank at his or her own discretion.

Depository Trust Company (DTC) An independent corporation owned by broker/dealers and banks responsible for (1) holding deposit securities owned by broker/dealers and banking institutions, (2) arranging the receipt and delivery of securities between users by means of debiting and crediting their respective accounts, (3) arranging for payment of monies between users in the settlement of transactions. The DTC is generally used by option writers because it guarantees delivery of underlying securities if assignment is made against securities held in DTC.

Depth (1) The amount of general investor interest in the market, comparing the number of issues traded with the number of issues listed: the more that are traded, the greater the "depth" of the market. (2) The "depth" of a security depends on how large a buy or sell order it can absorb without its price changing greatly.

Designated Concession An order for a number of securities given to a syndicate, which designates the concessions for the nonmembers of the account. For example, nonmember A gets 1,000 out of an order for 2,000 securities, nonmember B gets 750, and nonmember C gets 250.

Discount A term used to describe debt instruments trading at a price below their face values. For example, trading at 99 would mean that for $990 one could purchase a bond that would pay $1,000 principal at maturity.

Discount Bond A bond that sells in the marketplace at a price below its face value. See *Deep Discount Bond*.

Discount Broker A broker/dealer whose commission rates for buying and selling securities are markedly lower than those of a full-service broker. These brokers usually provide execution-only services.

Discount Note A note, originally sold at par, selling below its par value. A note is usually a government security.

Discount Rate (The) A rate of interest associated with borrowing reserves from a central bank by member banks in the Federal Reserve District. The rate is set by the officials of that central bank.

Discount Security A security sold on the basis of a bank rate discount. The investment return is realized solely from the accretion of this discounted amount to the security's maturity value. The most common type is a U.S. Treasury bill.

Discount Window A tellerlike cage at which member banks may borrow reserves from the Federal Reserve Bank upon pledge of acceptable collateral.

Distributor   See *Underwriter*.

Distribution   The sale of a large block of stock, through either an underwriting or an exchange distribution.

District Bank   One of the 12 Federal Reserve Banks acting as the central bank for its district.

District Business Conduct Committee   An NASD district subcommittee responsible for supervising and enforcing the Board of Governors' Rules of Fair Practice; it consists of the officials of the district committee itself.

District Committee   The governing body of each of the 13 districts of the NASD.

District Uniform Practices Committee   One of 13 district committees within the NASD whose function is the dissemination of information regarding the Uniform Practice Code.

Dollar Bonds   Corporate or municipal serial bonds that are denominated and that trade in currency values instead of as a percentage of face amount because of the relatively small amounts available for each maturity in the entire issue.

DNR   See *Do Not Reduce (DNR) Order*.

Do Not Reduce (DNR) Order   A limit order to buy, a stop order to sell, or a stop-limit order to sell that is not to be reduced by the amount of a cash dividend on the ex-dividend date because the customer specifically requested that it be entered that way.

Double-Barreled Bond   Usually municipal revenue bonds, secured by both a defined source of revenue plus the full faith and credit of an issuer with taxing powers. See *Overlapping Debt*.

Downgrade   Lowering a bond rating by a rating service, such as Moody's or Standard & Poor's.

Draft   A debt instrument payable on sight, or at a specific future time, upon presentation to a paying agent, usually a bank.

DTC   See *Depository Trust Company*.

Due-Diligence Meeting   A meeting between corporation officials and the underwriting group to (1) discuss the registration statement, (2) prepare a final prospectus, and (3) negotiate a formal underwriting agreement.

Dutch Auction   Auction in which the sellers offer down for a purchase instead of the buyers bidding up. This term is often used incorrectly to describe the weekly T-bill auction.

DVP   See *Delivery Versus Payment*.

Easy Money   A situation in which the Federal Reserve System allows banks to accumulate enough funds to lower interest rates and make borrowing easier. Easy money fosters economic growth and inflation. See *Tight Money.*

Edge Act   A 1919 federal law allowing commercial banks the right to conduct international business across state lines.

Edge Act Corporation   A federal- or state-chartered subsidiary involved with foreign lending operations. See *Edge Act.*

Effective Date   The date on which a security can be offered publicly if no deficiency letter is submitted to the issuer by the SEC. It is generally no earlier than the twentieth calendar day after filing the registration statement.

Effective Sale   A round-lot transaction consummated on the floor of the New York Stock Exchange after entry of an odd-lot order by a customer. Its price is used to determine the execution price for the odd-lot order after consideration of the dealer's fee. See *Differential.*

Either/Or Order   See *Alternative (Either/Or) Order.*

Electing Sale   The round-lot transaction that activates (triggers) a stop order.

Equipment Trust Bond   A serial bond collateralized by the machinery and/or equipment of the issuing corporation.

Equity   The ownership interest in a company of holders of its common and preferred stock.

Equivalent Bond Yield   A percentage used to express the comparison of the discount yield of money market securities with the coupon yield of government obligations.

Execution   Synonym for a transaction or trade between a buyer and seller.

Ex-Legal   In municipals trading, the absence of a bond counsel's legal opinion usually connected with the delivery of the securities in the secondary market.

Face Value   The redemption value of a bond or preferred stock appearing on the face of the certificate, unless that value is otherwise specified by the issuing corporation. Also sometimes referred to as par value.

Fair and Reasonable   See *Five Percent Guideline.*

Fair Market Value   The price, based on the current market value determined by supply and demand, for which a buyer and seller are willing to make a transaction.

Fair Treatment   Under the NASD Rules of Fair Practice, members have a business relationship with their customers and a fiduciary responsibility in handling their accounts.

Fannie Maes   See *Federal National Mortgage Association.*

FANS   See *Free Account Net Settlement.*

Farm Credit Banks   Banks set up to deal with the specific financial needs of farmers and their businesses.

Farmers Home Administration (FHA)   Agency set up by the federal Department of Agriculture empowered to make loans to farm owners or tenants to help finance the acquisition or improvement of farm properties. The FHA also helps to finance community facilities by making loans to qualified municipal issuers.

Fast Market   Term used to describe fast-paced activity in a class of listed options. If the exchange cannot control the market, new orders may be delayed.

Federal Funds   (1) The excess reserve balances of a member bank on deposit at a central bank in the Federal Reserve System. This money may be made available to eligible borrowers on a short-term basis. (2) Funds used for settlement of money market instruments and U.S. government securities transactions. (3) A term used to mean "same-day availability" of money. See *Clearinghouse Funds.*

Federal Funds Rate   A rate of interest associated with borrowing a member bank's excess reserves. The rate is determined by the forces of supply and demand.

Federal Home Loan Banks (FHLB)   A government-sponsored agency that finances the home-building industry with mortgage loans from monies raised on offerings of bond issues; interest on these bonds is free from state and local income taxes.

Federal Intermediate Credit Banks (FICB)   An agency under the supervision of the Farm Credit Administration that makes loans to agricultural credit and production associations, with revenues derived from five-year bond issues. The interest on those bonds is free from state and local income tax.

Federal Land Banks (FLB)   Government-sponsored corporations that arrange primary mortgages on farm properties for general agricultural purposes; interest on their bonds is exempt from state and municipal taxes.

Federal National Mortgage Association (FNMA)   A publicly owned, government-sponsored corporation that purchases and sells mortgages insured by the Federal Housing Administration (FHA) or Farmers Home Administration (FHA) or guaranteed by the Veterans Administration (VA). Interest on these bonds, called Fannie Maes, is fully taxable.

Federal Open Market Committee   See *Open Market Operations.*

Federal Reserve Bank   One of the banks forming the Federal Reserve System.

Federal Reserve Board (FRB)   A U.S. government agency empowered by Congress to regulate credit in the country. Its members are appointed by the president of the United States.

Federal Reserve Requirement   Each commercial bank must set aside a certain percentage of its deposits, as determined by the Federal Reserve, to limit its potential credit-granting capability.

Federal Reserve System   A system of Federal Reserve Banks in the United States forming 12 districts under the control of the Federal Reserve Board. These banks regulate the extension of credit as well as other banking activities.

FHLB   See *Federal Home Loan Banks.*

FICB   See *Federal Intermediate Credit Banks*

Fill-or-Kill (FOK) Order   An order that requires the immediate purchase or sale of a specified amount of stock, though not necessarily at one price. If the order cannot be filled immediately, it is automatically canceled (killed).

Firm Market (Price, Quote)   In the OTC market, a quotation on a given security rendered by a market maker at which he or she stands ready and able to trade immediately.

Five Percent Guideline   A general guideline established by the NASD Board of Governors to define "fair" in a random trading transaction; it is not a rule or regulation and is used only as a rough criterion for markups, markdowns, and commissions.

Flat   When accrued interest is not added to the contract price of bonds (that is, most income bonds and all obligations for which interest has been deferred) in a transaction, the bonds are said to be trading "flat."

FLB   See *Federal Land Banks.*

FNMA   See *Federal National Mortgage Association (FNMA).*

FOK Order   See *Fill-or-Kill Order.*

Fourth Market   A term referring to the trading of securities between investors without the use of broker/dealers.

FRB   See *Federal Reserve Board.*

Free Box   A bank vault or other secure location used to store fully paid customer securities. The depositories of the NCC and DTC serve as free boxes for many member firm customers.

"Free" Crowd   See *Active Bonds (The "Free" Crowd).*

Full Disclosure Act   See *Securities Act of 1933.*

Fully Registered Bonds   Bonds registered as to both principal and interest.

Funded Debt   The aggregate of a corporation's liabilities with maturities exceeding five years.

General Obligation (GO) Bond   A tax-exempt bond whose pledge is the issuer's good faith and full taxing power.

Gilt-Edged   A security (bonds more often than stocks) that consistently pays dividends or interest.

Ginnie Maes   See *Government National Mortgage Association.*

Go-Around   A process by which the Federal Open Market Committee gathers bids and offers from primary bank and nonbank dealers.

Going Away   A term applied to the purchase of one or more serial maturities of an issue either by institution or by a dealer.

Going Private   Moving a company's shares from public to private ownership, either through an outside private investor or by the repurchase of shares. A company usually decides to go private when its shares are selling way below book value.

Going Public   A private company is "going public" when it first offers its shares to the investing public.

Good Delivery   Proper delivery by a selling firm to the purchaser's office of certificates that are negotiable without additional documentation and that are in units acceptable under the Uniform Practice Code.

Good-Faith Deposit   An amount of money given by members of an underwriting syndicate to the syndicate manager to guarantee their financial performance under the syndicate agreement.

Good Money   Another term for federal funds.

Good-till-Canceled (GTC or Open) Order   An order to buy or sell that remains valid until executed or canceled by the customer.

Government National Mortgage Association (GNMA)   An offshoot of the FNMA, a wholly owned government corporation (operated by the Department of Housing and Urban Development, HUD) that provides primary mortgages through bond issuances carrying no tax exemptions. GNMA securities are called "Ginnie Maes."

Green Shoe   In an underwriting agreement, a clause that allows the syndicate to purchase additional shares at the same price as the original offering. This lessens the risk for the syndicate.

Group Sales   Sales of securities by a syndicate manager to institutional purchasers from "the pot."

GTC See *Good-till-Canceled (GTC or Open) Order.*

Guaranteed Bonds Bonds issued by a subsidairy corporation and guaranteed as to principal and/or interest by the parent corporation.

Hedge Any combination of long and/or short positions taken in securities, options, or commodities in which one position tends to reduce the risk of the other.

Hit the Bid Term applied to the situation in which a seller accepts the buyer's highest bid. For example, if the ask price is 34¼ and the bid is 34, the seller "hits the bid" by accepting 34.

Hot Issue A security that is expected to trade in the aftermarket at a premium over the public offering price.

House On the street, a firm or individual engaged in business as a broker/dealer or investment banker.

House Account An account managed by a firm executive and/or handled at the firm's main office. No salesperson receives a commission on transactions in a house account.

Housing Authority Bond A municipal bond whose payment of interest and/or principal is contingent upon the collection of rents and other fees from users of a housing facility built with the proceeds of the issuance of the bond.

Immediate or Cancel (IOC) Order An order that requires immediate execution at a specified price of all or part of a specified amount of stock: the unexecuted portion has to be canceled by the broker.

Inactive Bonds Debt instruments that are expected by the NYSE Floor Department to trade only infrequently. All bids and offers, therefore, are filed in a "cabinet" or "can" (on cards colored to reflect effective lifetimes) until they are canceled or executed.

Inactive Market See *Narrow Market.*

Income (Adjustment) Bonds In the event of bankruptcy, long-term debt obligations are offered in exchange for outstanding bonds by the court-appointed receiver. The interest requirement associated with such debt will be paid by the corporation only when, as, and if earned.

Indenture A written agreement between corporation and creditors containing the terms of a debt issue, such as rate of interest, means of payment, maturity date, terms of prior payment of principal, collateral, priorities of claims, trustee.

Indenture Qualification Statement For publicly offered debt instruments not subject to registration under the Securities Act of 1933 but subject to the Trust Indenture Act of 1939, the statement required to be filed with the SEC to comply with the latter act.

Indication of Interest   An expression of consideration by an underwriter's circle of customers for investment in a new security expected to be offered soon. It is not a binding commitment on the customer or the underwriter.

Industrial Development Bonds   Industrial revenue bonds issued to improve the environment and subject to certain Internal Revenue Service regulations with regard to the tax-exempt status of the interest payments.

Industrial Revenue Bonds   Municipal bonds issued for the purpose of constructing facilities for profit-making corporations. The tax-exempt feature of these bonds may be restricted by certain Internal Revenue Service regulations. The corporation, rather than the municipality, is liable for the payment of interest and principal.

Inflation   A general rise in prices.

Insider   An officer, director, or principal stockholder of a publicly owned corporation and members of their immediate families. This category may also include people who obtain nonpublic information about a company and use it for personal gain.

Institution   A large organization engaged in investing in securities, such as a bank, insurance company, mutual fund, or pension fund. An institutional broker buys and sells securities for any of the above dealing in large volumes and charging a lower-than-usual per-unit commission. An institutional investor is any of the foregoing institutions who buy and sell securities. An institutional house is any brokerage firm dealing with such institutions. Institutional sales are sales of any type of securities by such institutions.

Insubstantial Quantity   Under NASD interpretations regarding hot issues, $5,000 face value in bonds is considered an "insubstantial quantity." It may be allocated to certain restricted parties.

Interpositioning   An unethical and unfair practice by a broker/dealer of needlessly employing a third party between the customer and the best available market, so that the customer pays more on a purchase or receives less on a sale than he or she should.

In the Tank   Colloquial expression for a security or group of securities that is quickly losing value.

Intraday   Meaning "within the day," this term is most often used to describe daily high and low prices of a security or commodity.

Investment Adviser   A person, company, or institution registered with the SEC under the Investment Advisors Act of 1940 to manage the investment of third parties.

Investment Advisors Act of 1940   A federal law requiring those who charge a fee for investment advice to register with the SEC. Exceptions include banks, some brokers, and newspapers with broad-based readership.

Investment Banker   A broker/dealer organization that provides a service to industry through counsel, market making, and underwriting of securities.

Involuntary (Statutory) Underwriter   An individual or corporation that purchases an unregistered security and offers it in a public distribution without an effective registration statement. Such parties are subject to fine and/or imprisonment.

IOC Order   See *Immediate or Cancel (IOC) Order.*

Irredeemable Bond   (1) See *Perpetual Bond.* (2) A bond whose issuer does not have the right to redeem the bond before maturity.

Issue (Issuance)   (1) Any of a company's classes of securities. (2) The act of distributing securities.

Issuer   A corporation, trust, or governmental agency engaged in the distribution of its securities.

Jeeps   See *Graduated Payment Mortgages (GPM).*

Joint Account   An account including jointly two or more people.

Joint Tenants in Common   An account in which the two or more people participating have fractional interests in its assets. The interest percentage of the assets becomes part of each person's estate upon death.

Joint Tenants with Right of Survivorship (W/R/O/S)   An account in which two or more people have an ownership interest and whose assets are inherited by its survivors upon the death of any participant.

Junk Bond   Any bond with a Moody's or Standard & Poor's credit rating of BB or lower. Such bonds, usually issued by companies without long track records, can produce high yields.

Lead Manager   The member of an underwriting syndicate charged with the primary responsibility for conducting the affairs of the syndicate. See *Syndicate.*

Legal Delivery   A delivery of securities that is not good delivery because of the way in which registration of the certificates was carried out.

Letter Bonds　Privately sold bonds that are accompanied by an investment letter giving the investor the right to transfer or resell them.

Level Debt Service　A requirement in a municipality's charter that the annual debt service payment must be approximately equal— or "level"—each year. Its purpose is to budget effectively all tax revenues of that municipality.

Leverage　(1) In securities, increasing return without increasing investment. Buying stock on margin is an example. (2) In finance, the relationship of a firm's debt to its equity, as expressed in the debt-to-equity ratio. If the company earns a return on the borrowed money greater than the cost of the debt, it is successfully applying the principle of leverage.

Limit Price　A modification of an order to buy or sell. With a sell limit order, the customer is instructing the broker to make the sale at or above the limit price. With a buy limit order, the customer is instructing the broker to make the purchase at or below the limit price.

Liquidity　(1) The ability of the market in a particular security to absorb a reasonable amount of trading at reasonable price changes. Liquidity is one of the most important characteristics of a good market. (2) The relative ease with which investors can convert their securities into cash.

Listed Bond Table　A daily publication appearing in many newspapers showing a summary of transactions by exchange or, if OTC, by security.

Long Market Value　The market value of securities owned by a customer (long in his or her account).

Long Position　The ownership of securities.

Long-Term Debt　The debt of a company due and payable more than one year hence.

M　(1) Abbreviation for 1,000. For example, "5M" means 5,000; "25M" means 25,000. Usually used to denote the face value of a bond. (2) Preceding the name of a stock in the National Quotation Bureau's daily Pink Sheet, the security can be margined.

M1　The nation's money supply, defined as total currency in circulation plus all demand deposits in commercial banks.

M2　M1 plus savings and time deposits of less than $100,000 in commercial banks.

Major Bracket Participant   A member of an underwriting syndicate who will handle a large part of the issue in relation to other members of the syndicate.

Mandatory Redemption Account   See *Bond Amortization Fund*.

Manipulation   Making securities prices rise or fall artificially, through aggressive buying or selling by one investor in connection with others. This is a severe violation of federal securities laws.

Markdown   The fee charged by a broker/dealer acting as a dealer when he or she buys a security from a customer and sells it, at a higher price, to a market maker. The fee, or markdown, is included in the sale price and is not itemized separately in the confirmation. See *As Principal; Five Percent Guideline*.

Marketable Security   (1) A security that may be readily purchased or sold. (2) A U.S. government bond freely traded in the open market. See *Certificate of Indebtedness (CI); Treasury Bills; Treasury Bonds; Treasury Notes*.

Marketability   How easily a security can be bought and sold. See *Liquidity*.

Market-if-Touched Order   An order allowable only on the CBOE. Such a buy order is activated when a series declines to a predetermined price or below. Such a sell order is activated when a series rises to a predetermined price or higher.

Market Maker   (1) An options exchange member who trades for his or her own account and risk. This member is charged with the responsibility of trading so as to maintain a fair, orderly, and competitive market. He or she may not act as agent. (2) A firm actively making bids and offers in the OTC market.

Market Not Held Order   An order to buy or sell securities at the current market with the investor leaving the exact timing of its execution up to the floor broker. If the floor broker is holding a "market not held" buy order and the price could decline, he or she may wait to buy when a better price becomes available. There is no guarantee for the investor that a "market not held" order will be filled.

Market Order   An order to be executed immediately at the best available price.

Market Price   (1) The last reported sale price for an exchange-traded security. (2) For over-the-counter securities, a consensus among market makers.

Market Tone   The "health" of a market. The tone is good when dealers and market makers are actively trading on narrow spreads. It is poor when trading drops off and spreads widen.

Market Value   The price that would be paid for a security or other asset.

Markup   The fee charged by a broker/dealer acting as a dealer when he or she buys a security from a market maker and sells it to a customer at a higher price. The fee, or markup, is included in the sale price and is not itemized separately in the confirmation. See *As Principal; Five Percent Guideline.*

Matched Sale/Purchase Transaction (Reverse Repurchase Agreement)   A Federal Open Market Committee sale of Treasury bills or other government securities for cash settlement with a provision for repurchase at the same price plus interest on a specific date in the future.

Maturity (Date)   The date on which a loan, bond, or debenture comes due; both principal and any accrued interest due must be paid.

Maturity Value   The amount an investor receives when a security is redeemed at maturity; not including any periodic interest payments. This value usually equals the par value, although on zero-coupon, compound interest, and multiplier bonds, the principal amount of the security at issuance plus the accumulated investment return on the security is included.

Member Bank   A bank that is a member of the Federal Reserve System. Member banks must purchase stock in the Federal Reserve Bank in their district equal to 6% of their own paid-in capital.

Member Takedown   A situation in which a syndicate member buys bonds at the takedown (or member's discount) and then sells them to a customer at the public offering price.

Missing the Market   The failure by a member of the exchange to execute an order due to his or her negligence. The member is obliged to reimburse promptly the customer for any losses due to the mistake.

Monetary Supply   See *M1; M2.*

Money   Coin or certificates generally accepted in payment of debts for goods and services.

Money Market   The market for dealers who trade riskless, short-term securities; T-bills, certificates of deposits, banker's acceptances, and commercial paper.

Money Market Fund   Name for an open-ended investment company whose portfolio consists of money market securities.

Money Market Instruments   Short-term debt (of less than one year to maturity) usually issued at a discount and not bearing interest. For example, Treasury bills, commercial paper, or banker's acceptances.

Money Supply   See *M1; M2.*

Moody's Investors Service   One of the best-known bond rating agencies, owned by Dun & Bradstreet. *Moody's Investment Grade* assigns letter grades to bonds based on their predicted long-term yield (Aaa, Aa, A, etc.) Moody's also rates commercial paper, municipal short-term issues, and preferred and common stocks. Another publication is a six-volume annual, with weekly or semiweekly supplements, giving great detail on issuers and securities. Publications include *Moody's Bond Record* and *Moody's Bond Survey.* Moody's investment ratings are considered the norm for investment decisions by fiduciaries.

Moral Suasion   An expression used to denote the Federal Reserve Board's ability to influence member bank financial policies by threatening to employ drastic powers to gain compliance with its own preferences.

Mortgage-Backed Security (MBS)   A security (1) that is issued by the Federal Home Loan Mortgage Corporation, the Federal National Mortgage Association, or the Government National Mortgage Association and (2) that is backed by mortgages payments to investors that are received out of the interest and principal of the underlying mortgages.

Mortgage Bond   The most prevalent type of secured corporate bond. The bondholders are protected by the pledge of the corporation's real assets evaluated at the time of issuance. See *Open-End Provision.*

Mortgage Pool   A group, or "pool," or mortgages on the same class of property, with the same interest rate and the same maturity date.

Mortgage REIT   A REIT primarily engaged in the financing of new construction.

MSRB   See *Municipal Securities Rulemaking Board.*

Municipal Bond (Security)   Issued by a state or local government, a debt obligation whose funds either may support a government's general financing needs or may be spent on special projects. Municipal bonds are free from federal tax on the accrued interest and also free from state and local taxes if issued in the state of residence.

Municipal Securities Rulemaking Board (MSRB)   Registered under the Maloney Act in 1975, the board consists of industry and public representatives. It is designed to create rules and regulations for municipal bond trading among brokers, dealers, and banks. Its powers are similar to those of the NASD.

Munifacts   A private communications network originating in the New York offices of *The Bond Buyer*. It transmits current bond market information to subscribers.

Mutilation   A term used to describe the physical condition of a certificate, note, bond, or coupon when the instrument is no longer considered negotiable. The standards for determining what is mutilated are set forth in MSRB rule G-12(e) (ix). Such missing items as the signature of the authorized officer, the serial number of the instrument, the amount or the payable date would cause the instrument to be considered mutilated. The issuing authority, or its agent, must be contacted to obtain certain documents needed to make the instrument negotiable again.

N   "Note" when used in lowercase with a U.S. government bid-asked quotation.

Narrowing the Spread   The action taken by a broker/deaker to narrow the spread between bids and offers, by bidding higher or offering lower than the previous bid or offer. Also called closing the market.

Narrow Market   Light trading and great price fluctuations with regard to the volume on a securities or commodities market. Also known as thin market and inactive market.

NASD   See *National Association of Securities Dealers*.

NASDAQ   See *National Association of Securities Dealers Automated Quotations*.

NASDAQ OTC Price Index   See *National Association of Securities Dealers Automated Quotations Over-the-Counter Price Index*.

NASD Code of Arbitration   Code governing the arbitration of controversies arising out of, and relating exclusively to, securities transactions. This code is available for disputes between members of the National Association of Securities Dealers or between customers and NASD members.

NASD Code of Procedure   Code prescribed by the Board of Governors of the National Association of Securities Dealers for the administration of disciplinary proceedings stemming from infractions of the Rules of Fair Practice.

National Association of Securities Dealers (NASD)   An association of broker/dealers in over-the-counter securities organized on a nonprofit, non–stock-issuing basis. Its general aim is to protect investors in the OTC market.

National Association of Securities Dealers Automated Quotation System (NASDAQ) A computerized quotations network by which NASD members can communicate bids and offers to each other.

Level 1 Provides only the arithmetic mean of the bids and offers entered by members.

Level 2 Provides the individual bids and offers next to the name of the member entering the information.

Level 3 Available to NASD members only, enables the member to enter bids and offers and receive Level 2 service.

National Association of Securities Dealers Automated Quotations Over-the-Counter Price Index A computer-oriented, broad-based indicator of activity in the unlisted securities market, updated every five minutes.

National Clearing Corporation (NCC) An NASD affiliate organization responsible for arranging a daily clearance of transactions for members by means of a continuous net settlement process. Although its principal office is in New York City, it operates electronic satellite branches in major U.S. cities.

National Institutional Delivery System (NIDS) A system of automated transmissions of confirmation from a dealer to an institutional investor and the affirmation and book-entry settlement of the transaction. MSRB rules state that NIDS must be used on certain transactions between dealers and customers. Also known as "institutional delivery" or ID for short.

National Quotation Bureau, Inc. (NQB) A subsidiary of Commerce Clearing House, Inc., that distributes to subscribers several lists a day of broker/dealers making bids and/or offerings of securities traded over-the-counter. Also known as Pink Sheets.

National Quotations Committee A national committee of NASD that sets minimum standards for the publication of quotations furnished to newspapers, radio, or television.

Near Money A bond whose redemption date is near.

Negotiability In reference to securities, the ability to easily transfer title upon delivery.

Negotiable Paper or Instrument An order or promise to pay an amount of money that is easily transferable from one person to another, such as a check, promissory note, or draft.

Negotiated Bid   A bid on an underwriting that is negotiated by the issuer and a single underwriting syndicate. See *Competitive Bidding*.

Negotiated Marketplace   The over-the-counter market, in which transactions are negotiated between two parties. The opposite of auction marketplace.

Negotiated Underwriting   The underwriting of new securities issues in which the spread purchase price and the public offering price are determined through negotiation rather than through bidding. See *Negotiated Bid*.

Net Interest Cost   The net cost to the issuer of a debt instrument, taking into account both the coupon and the discount or premium on the issue.

New Issue   (1) Any authorized but previously unissued security offered for sale by an issuer. (2) The resale of treasury shares.

New Money   The issue of new bonds with a greater par value than that of bonds being called or maturing.

New York Plan   A method of issuing equipment trust certificates (serial debt obligations issued by airlines, railroads, and other common carriers) to acquire equipment. See *Philadelphia Plan*.

Next-Day Contract   A security transaction calling for settlement the day after trade date.

NH   See *Not Held (NH) Order*.

Nominal Quotation   A quotation that is an approximation of the price that could be expected on a purchase or sale and that is not to be considered firm in the event that a purchase or sale is consummated. See *Numbers Only*.

Nominal Value   See *Face Value*.

Nominal Yield   The annual interest rate payable on a bond, specified in the indenture and printed on the face of the certificate itself. Also known as coupon yield.

Normal Trading Unit   The accepted unit of trading in a given marketplace: for NASDAQ-traded securities, it is $10,000 par value for bonds. See *Odd Lots; Round Lots*.

Normal Yield Curve   A graph that plots the yield of equivalent securities with different maturities at any given point in time. A normal yield curve indicates that short-term securities have lower interest rates than long-term securities.

Not Held (NH) Order   An order that does not hold the executing member financially responsible for using his or her personal judgment in the execution price or time of a transaction. See *Market Not Held Over*.

Notice of Redemption The announcement of an issuer's intention to call bonds prior to their dates of maturity.

Numbers Only A dealer's response to a request for a quote with just numbers; the dealer is not obligated to make a transaction. See *Nominal Quotation*.

Odd Lot An amount of stock less than the normal trading unit. See *Round Lot*.

Off-Board An expression that may refer to transactions over the counter in unlisted securities or to transactions involving listed bonds or shares that were not executed on a national securities exchange.

Offer The price at which a person is ready to sell. See *Bid-and-Ask Quotation (or Quote)*.

Offering (Asked) Price The lowest price available for a round lot.

Offering Circular (1) A publication that is prepared by the underwriters and that discloses basic information about an issue of securities to be offered in the primary market. (2) Sometimes used to describe a document used by dealers when selling large blocks of stock in the secondary market.

Offering Date When a security is first offered for public sale.

Offering Scale The price, expressed in eighths of a point or in decimals, at which the underwriter will sell the individual serial maturities of a bond issue.

Offer Wanted (OW) Notation made, usually in the Pink or Yellow Sheets, by a broker/dealer who wants another dealer to make an offer for a security.

Official Notice of Sale An advertisement issued by a municipal issuer to solicit competitive bids for an upcoming municipal bond issue. It usually includes all the facts about the issue and appears in the *Daily Bond Buyer*.

Open Market Operations The activity of the federal Open Market Committee, in behalf of the Federal Reserve Banking System, to arrange outright purchases and sales of government and agency securities, match sale/purchase agreements, and repurchase agreements to promote the monetary policy of the Federal Reserve Board.

Open Order See *Good-till-Canceled (GTC or Open) Order*.

Operating Income Net sales less cost of sales, selling expenses, administrative expenses, and depreciation. The pretax income from normal operations.

Operations Department   A department of the NYSE responsible for (1) the listing and delisting of corporate and government securities and (2) all trading activity and ancillary services.

Order Department   A group that routes buy and sell instructions to the trading floors of the appropriate stock exchanges and executes orders in the OTC market for trading accounts of both firms and customers.

Out for a Bid   In the municipal bond market, the securities are "out for a bid" when a dealer lends them to an agent who then attempts to sell them.

Outright Purchases or Sales   The net purchases or sales made by the Federal Open Market Committee, including buys and sells that may be partially offset by repo or reverse repo agreements.

Overlapping Debt   A bond having two issuers. See *Double-Barreled Bond*.

Overnight Position   The investory in a security at the end of a trading day.

Over-the-Counter Option (OTC)   A market for securities, conducted mainly over the telephone, made up of dealers who may or may not be members of a securities exchange. Thousands of companies have insufficient shares outstanding, stockholders, or earnings to warrant listing on a national exchange. Securities of these companies are therefore traded in the over-the-counter market between dealers who act either as agents for their customers or as principals. The over-the-counter market is the principal market for U.S. government and municipal bonds and for stocks of banks and insurance companies.

Overtrading   A practice in violation of NASD principles. A broker/dealer overpays a customer for a security to enable the customer to subscribe to another security offered by that broker/dealer at a higher markup than the loss to be sustained when the firm sells the customer's first security at prevailing market prices.

Overvalued   In securities trading, a security whose market price is higher than it should be in the opinion of fundamental analysts. See *Fair Value; Undervalued*.

OW   See *Offer Wanted*.

Paper   Relatively short-term debt securities.

Parity Bonds   Any two or more issues having the same priority of claim or lien against pledged revenues.

Parking   The practice by a dealer of selling a security to another dealer to reduce the seller's net capital requirement. The securities are sold back to the first dealer when a buyer is found, and the second dealer recoups any carrying charges.

Partial Delivery   A delivery of fewer securities than the amount contracted for in the sales transactions.

Participate but Do Not Initiate (PNI) Order   On large orders to buy or sell, an instruction given to a broker from institutional buyers or sellers not to initiate a new price, but either to let the market create a new price or obtain a favorable price through gradual and intermittent transactions. This allows the buyers or sellers to accumulate or distribute shares without disturbing the market forces. This could also be done by institutions that are not permitted by law to create an uptick or a downtick in the market.

Pass-through Security (P/T)   A debt security representing an interest in a pool of mortgages requiring monthly payments composed of interest on unpaid principal and a partial repayment of principal. Thus the payments are passed through the intermediaries, from the debtors to investors.

Par (Value)   The face amount or nominal value of a security. For preferred stocks, par value has importance insofar as it signifies the dollar value on which the dividend/interest is figured and the amount to be repaid upon redemption. Preferred dividends are usually expressed as a percentage of the stock's par value. The interest on bonds is expressed as a percentage of the bond's par value. See *Face Value*.

Pegging   Also known as stabilization. Keeping a security's offer price at a certain level by means of a bid at or slightly below the price. Pegging is legal only in underwriting.

Penalty Syndicate Bid   A series of restrictive financial measures written into agreements among underwriters with the purpose of discouraging resale of securities requiring stabilization. A monetary penalty helps to ensure distribution to investment portfolios and not to traders and speculators seeking short-term profits at the expense of the underwriters.

Perpetual Bond   A bond with no maturity date. Also called an annuity bond.

Philadelphia Plan   The issuance of equipment trust bonds in which the title to the leased equipment remains with the trustee until all the outstanding serial maturities for the issue are retired. It would then pass to the leasing issuer of the securities. See *New York Plan.*

Pickup   The increased yield (usually small) achieved by means of a swap of bonds with similar coupon rates and maturities at a basis price.

Picture   The prices at which a broker/dealer or specialist is ready to trade. For example, "The picture on XYZ is 18½ to 19, 1,000 either way."

Pink Sheets   A list of securities being traded by over-the-counter market makers, published every business day by the National Quotations Bureau. Equity securities are published separately on long Pink Sheets. Debt securities are published separately on long Yellow Sheets.

Pledged Revenues   Monies needed for—that is, pledged to—the payment of debt service and other deposits required by a bond contract. A net pledge or net revenue pledge is a pledge that all funds remaining after certain operational and maintenance costs are paid will be used for payment of debt services. A gross pledge or gross revenue pledge states that all revenues received will be used for the debt service prior to any deductions for costs or expenses.

PNI Order   See *Participate but Do Not Initiate (PNI) Order.*

Point   Since a bond is quoted as a percentage of $1,000, it means $10. For example, a municipal security discounted at 3½ points equals $35. It is quoted at 96½ or $965 per $1,000.

Pool   A group of debt instruments in which undivided interest is represented by another security.

Portfolio   Holdings of securities by an individual or institution. A portfolio may include preferred and common stocks, as well as bonds, of various enterprises.

POS   See *Preliminary Official Statement.*

Position   (1) The status of securities in an account—long or short. (2) To buy or sell a block of securities so that a position is established. (3) A dealer's inventory.

Pot, The   A pool of securities, aside from those distributed among individual syndicate members, that is allocated by the manager for group or institutional sales. When "the pot is clean," the

portion of the issue reserved for institutional (group) sales has
been completely sold.

Pot is Clean   See *Pot, The.*

Preliminary Agreement   An agreement between an issuing corporation and an underwriter drawn up prior to the effective date
and pending a decision by the underwriter on the success potential of the new securities. See *Indication of Interest.*

Preliminary Official Statement (POS)   Also known as the preliminary prospectus, the preliminary version or draft of an official
statement, as issued by the underwriters or issuers and subject
to change prior to the confirmation of offering prices or interest
rates. It is the only form of communication allowed between a
broker and prospective buyer before the effective date, usually
to gauge the interest of underwriters. Offers of sale or acceptance are not accepted on the basis of a preliminary statement.
A statement to that effect, printed in red, appears vertically on
the face of the document. This caveat, required by the Securities
Act of 1933, is what gives the document its nickname, "red herring."

Preliminary Prospectus   See *Preliminary Official Statement (POS).*

Premium   The amount by which the price paid for a preferred security exceeds its face value. The market price of a bond selling
at a price above its face amount.

Presold Issue   A completely sold-out issue of municipal or government securities prior to the announcement of its price or coupon
rate. This practice is illegal with regard to registered corporate
offerings, but it is not illegal in the primary distribution of municipals or Treasuries.

Primary Distribution (Offering)   The original sale of a company's
securities. The sale of authorized but unissued shares of stock
is a primary sale, while the resale of treasury shares is a secondary sale.

Primary Market   (1) Organized stock exchanges. (2) The new issue
market as opposed to the secondary market.

Prime Rate   The interest rate charged by a bank on loans made to
its most creditworthy customers.

Principal   See *As Principal.*

Principal Trade (Transaction)   Any transaction in which the dealer
or dealer bank effecting the trade takes over ownership of the
securities.

Principal Value   The face value of an obligation that must be repaid at maturity and that is separate from interest. Often called simply "principal."

Prior Issue   (1) Term applied to an outstanding issue of bonds when they are to be refinanced by a refunding. (2) Previous bond issues that normally possess a first, or senior, lien on pledged revenues.

Prior Lien Bond   A bond that takes precedence over all the other bonds from the issuer because they hold a higher-priority claim. These bonds are usually issued as a result of reorganizations arising from bankruptcy proceedings.

Prospectus   A document that contains material information for an impending offer of securities (containing most of the information included in the registration statement) and that is used for solicitation purposes by the issuer and underwriters.

Prudent Man Investing   Investing in a fashion that is exemplified by the conduct of a conservative person managing his or her own assets. In certain cases this type of investing is limited to "legal list." Some states use the "prudent man" rule as a legal guideline for investing others' money.

Public Offering (Distribution)   The offering of securities for sale by an issuer.

Purchase Group   Investment bankers who, as a group, purchase a new issue for resale to the public. The purchase group (or syndicate) differs from the selling group, another group of investment bankers whose function is distribution. See *Syndicate; Underwriting Agreement.*

Qualified Legal Opinion   A conditional affirmation of a security's legality, which is given before or after the security is sold. An unqualified legal opinion (called a clean opinion) is an unconditional affirmation of the legality of securities.

Quotation or Quote   See *Bid-and-Asked Quotation (or Quote).*

RAN   See *Revenue Anticipation Note.*

Range   A set of prices consisting of the opening sale, high sale, low sale, and latest sale of the day for a given security.

Rate of Return   See *Current Yield, Yield to Maturity.*

Rating Agencies   Organizations that publicly rate the credit quality of securities issuers, the most often cited being Moody's Investor's Services, Inc., and Standard & Poor's Corporation.

Receiver's Certificates   Short-term (90- to 120-day) debt obligations issued by a receiver for a bankrupt corporation to supply working capital during the receiver's inquiry. These obligations take priority over the claims of all other creditors.

Reciprocal Immunity Doctrine   A court decision that neither the federal government nor states can tax income received from securities issued by the other. A state cannot tax income from Treasury securities or federal agency obligations, and the federal government cannot tax income from state-issued securities.

Red Book   See *Dealer Book*.

Redemption   For bonds, the retirement of the securities by repayment of face value or above (that is, at a premium price) to their holders.

Redemption Notice   A publicly issued notice stating an issuer's intent to redeem securities.

Redemption Provision   See *Catastrophe (Calamity) Call*.

Red Herring   See *Preliminary Official Statement (POS)*.

Rediscount   A situation in which a member bank of the Federal Reserve System borrows funds from the Federal Reserve using eligible collateral. This collateral, in turn, came from one of the bank's borrowers.

Refunding (Refinancing)   The issuance of a new debt security, using the proceeds to redeem either older bonds at maturity or outstanding bonds issued under less favorable terms and conditions.

Registered as to Interest Only   Bonds that are registered as to interest and on which interest checks are sent to the registered owner, but that are payable to the bearer at maturity.

Registered as to Principal Only   Bonds that are registered and that are payable at maturity to the registered holder, but that have coupons attached that must be presented by the bearer periodically for payment.

Registered Bond   An outstanding bond whose owner's name is recorded on the books of the issuing corporations. Legal title may be transferred only when the bond is endorsed by the registered owner.

Registered Representative   See *Account Executive*.

Registered Security   (1) A certificate clearly inscribed with the owner's name. (2) A bond that is registered with the SEC at the time of its sale. If such an initial registration does not take place, then the term also includes any security sold publicly and in accordance with the SEC's rules.

Registration Statement   A document required to be filed with the

SEC by the issuer of securities before a public offering may be attempted. The Securities Act of 1933 mandates that it contain all material and accurate facts. Such a statement is required also when affiliated persons intend offering sizable amounts of securities. The SEC examines the statement for a 20-day period, seeking obvious omissions or misrepresentations of fact.

Regular Way Contract   The most frequently used delivery contract. For stocks and corporate and municipal bonds, this type of contract calls for delivery on the fifth business day after the trade. For U.S. government bonds and options, delivery must be made on the first business day after the trade.

Regulation G   A Federal Reserve Board regulation requiring any person, other than a bank or broker/dealer, who extends credit secured directly or indirectly with margin securities, to register and be subject to Federal Reserve Board jurisdiction.

Regulation Q   The Federal Reserve Board's interest rate on time deposits.

Regulation T   A Federal Reserve Board regulation that explains the conduct and operation of general and special accounts within the offices of a broker/dealer firm, prescribing a code of conduct for the effective use and supervision of credit.

Regulation U   A Federal Reserve Board regulation that regulates the extension of credit by banks when securities are used as collateral.

Regulation W   The regulation of the Federal Reserve Board pertaining to installment loans.

Regulation X   A set of rules established by the Federal Reserve Board that places equal burdens of responsibility for compliance with Regulations G, T, and U on the borrower as well as the lender.

Reoffering Sale   Listed by date of maturity, the prices and yields of securities offered by the underwriters.

Reopening an Issue   The offering by the Treasury of additional securities in an issue that's been already offered and sold. The new securities have the same terms and conditions, but they sell at the prevailing prices.

Repo   See *Repurchase Agreement.*

Representations to Management   When any member of the NYSE or person associated with a member wishes to represent a corporation or its stockholders, that person must meet certain rules established by the exchange.

Repurchase Agreement (Repo)   (1) A Federal Open Market Committee arrangement with a dealer in which it contracts to purchase a government or agency security at a fixed price, with provision for its resale at the same price at a rate of interest determined competitively. Used by dealers in government and municipal securities to reduce carrying costs. This transaction is not legal for nonexempt securities. (2) A method of financing inventory positions by sale to a nonbank institution with the agreement to buy the position back.

Reserve City Bank   A commercial bank with its main office in a city where a central bank or branch is located that has net demand deposits exceeding $400 million.

Reserve Requirement   The obligation of a commercial bank to set aside and refrain from lending a percentage of its available currency. This is a form of protection for depositors.

Retention   The portion of an underwriter's takedown for sale to its customers. The syndicate manager holds back the balance of the takedown for institutional sales and for allocation to selling group firms that are not syndicate members.

Retirement of Debt Securities   The repayment of principal and accrued interest due to the holders of a bond issue.

Return   See *Yield (Rate of Return).*

Revenue Anticipation Note (RAN)   A short-term municipal debt instrument usually offered on a discount basis. Proceeds of future revenues are pledged as collateral to the payment of the note at maturity.

Revenue Bonds   Tax-exempted bonds whose interest payments are dependent upon, secured by, and redeemable from the income generated by a particular project financed by their issuance.

Reverse a Swap   The transaction following a bond swap that reinstates the original portfolio position—reversing the swap.

Reversal Arbitrage   A riskless arbitrage involving the sale of the stock short, the writing of a put, and the purchase of a call with the options all having the same terms. See *Conversion Arbitrage.*

Reverse Repurchase Agreement (Reverse Repo)   (1) For Federal Open Market Committee transactions, synonymous with matched sale/purchase agreements. (2) A transaction by which a broker/dealer provides funds to customers by means of purchasing a security with a contract to resell it at the same price plus interest.

Risk Arbitrage   A purchase and short sale of potentially equal securities at prices that may realize a profit. See *Bona Fide Arbitrage.*

Round Lot   A unit of trading or a multiple thereof. On the NYSE,
stocks are traded in round lots of 100 shares for active stocks
and 10 shares for inactive ones. Bonds are traded in units of
$1,000. See *Normal Trading Unit; Odd Lot.*

Rules of Fair Practice   A set of rules established and maintained by
the NASD Board of Governors regulating the ethics employed
by members in the conduct of their business.

Run   A market maker's list of offerings, including bid-offer prices
(and, for bonds, par values and prices).

Run on a Bank   A situation in which a substantial number of depositors, fearing for the safety of their funds, seek withdrawal
of their balances in currency.

Running Through the Pot   In a distribution, the syndicate manager
can take securities back from the group members and put them
into "the pot" for institutional sales. Usually this is done if institutional sales are doing better than retail sales. See *Pot, The.*

Savings Bank   A state-chartered institution that accepts both time
and demand deposits. Usually organized as a stock or mutual
company, it uses its deposits to invest in mortgages, real estate,
government bonds, and so on.

Savings Bond   Bond issued through the U.S. government at a discount and in face values from $50 to $10,000. The interest is
exempt from state and local taxes, and no federal tax comes due
until the bond is redeemed. See *Series EE (Savings) Bonds; Series
HH (Current Income) Bond.*

Savings Deposit   An interest-earning deposit in a commercial bank
subject to immediate withdrawal.

Scale   When serial bonds are initially offered, the scale designates
the various maturity dates, the coupon rates, and the offering
prices.

Scale Orders   Multiple limit orders entered by investors at various
prices but at the same time. The purpose is to obtain an overall,
or average, favorable purchase or sale price. Multiples of round
lots may be either bought at prices scaled down from a given
value or sold at prices scaled up from a given value.

Scalper   A market maker who puts heavy markups or markdowns
on transactions. See *Five Percent Guideline.*

Seasoned Issue An issue, once distributed, that trades actively and that has great liquidity.

Secondary Market (1) A term referring to the trading of securities not listed on an organized exchanged. (2) A term used to describe the trading of securities subsequent to their primary offering.

Secured Obligation (Bond/Debt) A debt whose payment of interest and/or principal is secured by the pledge of physical assets.

Securities Act of 1933 Federal legislation designed to protect the public in the issuance and distribution of securities by providing to prospective purchasers full and accurate information about an issue.

Securities and Exchange Commission (SEC) A government agency responsible for the supervision and regulation of the securities industry.

Securities Exchange Act of 1934 Federal legislation designed to protect the public against unfair and inequitable practices on stock exchanges and in over-the-counter markets throughout the United States.

Securities Industry Association (SIA) An association devoted to instructing member employees and to lobbying for the members' interests.

Securities Industry Automation Corporation (SIAC) A corporation owned two-thirds by the New York Stock Exchange and one-third by the American Stock Exchange. The corporation is under contract to receive trade information from the two exchanges and from their members for the purpose of assisting in final settlement. Data are also supplied to the Consolidated Tape Association (CTA), the Consolidated Quotation System (CQS), the National Security Clearing Corporation (NSCC), and the Intermarket Trading System (ITS). To perform this function, SIAC issues balance orders and continuous net settlement information to the members.

Securities Investor Protection Corporation (SIPC) Formed by the Securities Investors Protection Act of 1970, a government-sponsored, private, nonprofit corporation that guarantees repayment of money and securities to customers in amounts up to $500,000 per customer in the event of a broker/dealer bankruptcy. SIPC covers up to a maximum of $500,000 only $100,000 of which may be for cash. If you have, for example,

$100,000 in cash and $100,000 in securities in your account, you are covered for $200,000 ($100,000 of which is cash). If you have $200,000 in securities and $200,000 in cash, you are covered for $300,000 ($200,000 in securities plus $100,000 in cash). If you have $500,000 in securities and $100,000 in cash, you are covered for $500,000, the maximum.

Security   A transferable instrument evidencing ownership or creditorship, such as a note; stock or bond; evidence of debt; interest or participation in a profit-sharing agreement; investment contract; voting trust certificate; fractional undivided interest in oil, gas, or other mineral rights; or any warrant to subscribe to, or purchase, any of the foregoing or other similar instruments.

Security Districts   Thirteen administrative districts throughout the United States established by the NASD. Each district is governed by a district committee and represented on the association's Board of Governors.

Security Ratings   Ratings set by rating services, such as Moody's, Standard & Poor's, or Fitch, denoting evaluations of the investment and credit risk attached to securities.

Seek a Market   Look to make or buy a sale.

Selling Group   Selected broker/dealers of the NASD who contract to act as selling agents for underwriters and who are compensated by a portion of the sales charge (selling concession) on newly issued stocks. They assume no financial liability for the unsold balance, but they do not share in profit from syndicate residuals.

Sell Stop Order   A memorandum that becomes a market order to sell if and when someone trades a round lot at or below the memorandum price.

Serial Bond   An issue that matures in relatively small amounts at stated periodic intervals.

Serial Issue   An issue of bonds with maturity dates spread out over several years.

Series EE (Savings) Bonds   Nontransferable U.S. government bonds that are issued in denominations of $50 to $10,000 at a discount from their face values and that mature at their face values.

Shop/Shopping the Street   (1) "Shop" is slang for the broker/dealer's office. (2) "Shop" or "shopping the street" means a broker/dealer's gathering quotations from OTC market makers to form a basis for negotiating a transaction. See *Firm Market; Subject Market; Workout Market.*

Short Sale The sale of a security that is not owned at the time of the trade, necessitating its purchase some time in the future to "cover" the sale. A short sale is made with the expectation that the stock value will decline, so that the sale will be eventually covered at a price lower than the original sale, thus realizing a profit. Before the sale is covered, the broker/dealer borrows stock (for which collateral is put up) to deliver on the settlement date.

Short-Stop (Limit) Order A memorandum that becomes a limit order to sell short when someone creates a round-lot transaction at or below the memorandum price (electing sale). The short sale may or may not be executed since the rules then require that it be sold at least one-eighth above the electing sale as well as high enough in value to satisfy the limit price.

Simple Interest Interest calculated only on the original principal.

Simultaneous (Riskless) Transaction A transaction in which the broker/dealer takes a position in a security only after receipt of an order from a customer, and only for the purpose of acting as principal so as to disguise his or her remuneration from the transaction.

Sinker Slang for a bond with a sinking fund. See *Sinking Fund*.

Sinking Fund (1) An annual reserve of capital required to be set aside out of current earnings to provide monies for retirement of an outstanding bond issue and, sometimes, preferred stock. Such a feature has a favorable effect on the market value of that issue. (2) A separate account in the overall sinking fund for monies used to redeem securities by open market purchase, by request for tenders or call, or in accordance with the redemption schedule in the bond contract.

Soft Market The market for securities with low demand.

Sold to You Term used by over-the-counter traders to confirm the acceptance of their offer.

Special Assessment Bond A municipal general obligation bond whose debt service is paid by a special tax or assessment on users of the facility.

Special Bond Account An account in which a customer may favorably finance a purchase (1) exempted securities or (2) nonconvertible bonds traded on registered stock exchanges in the United States. The account is defined in Regulation T.

Special Convertible Security Account An account used to finance activity in debt securities that are traded on a registered stock exchange and the (1) are convertible into a margin stock or (2) carry a warrant or right to subscribe to a margin stock. The account is defined in Regulation T.

Special Obligation Bond   A bond secured by a specific revenue source.

Special Tax Bond   A municipal bond whose payment of interest and/or principal is contingent upon the collection of a tax imposed against those who will benefit from the use of the funds obtained from the issuance of the bond.

Split Offering   (1) An offering combining both a primary and secondary distribution. (2) A municipal bond offering, part of which consists of serial bonds and part of which is made up of term bonds.

Split Rating   A term used to describe the situation in which a corporation has been given different credit ratings by differing services.

Sponsor   See *Underwriter.*

Spread   (1) The difference in value between the bid and offering prices. (2) Underwriting compensation.

Stabilization   The syndicate manager is empowered by the members of his group to maintain a bid in the aftermarket at or slightly below the public offering price, thus "stabilizing" the market and giving the syndicate and selling group members a reasonable chance of successfully disposing of their allocations. This practice is a legal exception to the manipulation practices outlawed by the Securities and Exchange Act of 1934.

Stagflation   The combination of sluggish economic growth, high unemployment, and high inflation.

Stagnation   (1) A period of low volume and inactive trading on a securities market. (2) The economic doldrums resulting from retarded economic growth.

Standard & Poor's (S&P) Corporation   A source of investment services, most famous for its Standard & Poor's rating of bonds and its composite index of 425 industrial, 20 transportation, and 55 public utility common stocks, called Standard & Poor's Index.

Standby Commitment   See *Standby Underwriting Agreement.*

Standby Underwriting Agreement   An agreement between an investment banker and a corporation whereby the banker agrees for a negotiated fee to purchase any or all shares offered as a subscription privilege (rights offering) that are not bought by the rights holders by the time the offer expires.

Statutory Underwriter See *Involuntary (Statutory) Underwriter.*

Stickering Changing the official statement of a new issue by printing the altered information on adhesive-backed paper and
"stickering" onto the statement.

Sticky Deal An underwriting that, for one reason or another, will
be hard to market.

Stop-Limit Order A memorandum that becomes a limit (as opposed to a market) order immediately after a transaction takes
place at or through the indicated (memorandum) price.

Stop-Loss Order A customer's order to set the sell price of a stock
below the market price, thus locking in profits or preventing
further losses.

Stop Order A memorandum that becomes a market order only if
a transaction takes place at or through the price stated in the
memorandum. Buy stop orders are placed below it. The sale
that activates the memorandum is called the electing (activating
or triggering) sale. See *Buy Stop Order; Market Order; Sell Stop
Order.*

Stop-out Price The lower dollar price at auction for which Treasury bills are sold.

Stopped Out An expression reflecting a broker's unsuccessful attempt to improve upon the price of a transaction after having
been guaranteed an execution price by the specialist.

Street "Wall Street"—that is, the New York financial community,
as well as the exchanges throughout the country. The term is
becoming somewhat archaic, given the global nature of trading
today.

Subject Market (Price, Quote) In the OTC market, a range of buying or selling prices quoted by market makers at which they are
unable to trade immediately. Such prices are subject to verifi-
cation by the parties whose market they represent.

Subordinated Debt Instruments A debt instrument requiring that
repayment of principal may not be made until another debt instrument senior to it has been repaid in full.

Substitution (Swap) The sale of one security in an account to use
the proceeds to pay for the purchase of another security on the
same trade date. See *Switch (Contingent or Swap) Order.*

Suitability The appropriateness of a strategy or transaction, in light
of an investor's financial means and investment objectives.

Sweetener A special feature in a securities offering, such as convertibility, that encourages the purchase of the security.

Switch (Contingent or Swap) Order An order to buy one security and then sell another at a limit, or to sell one security and then to buy another at a limit. The transaction may also be called a proceeds sale if, as is usually the case, the proceeds of the sell order are applied against the expenses of the buy order.

Syndicate   A group of investment bankers who purchase securities from the issuer and then reoffer them to the public at a fixed price. The syndicate is usually organized along historical or social lines, with one member acting as syndicate manager, who ensures the successful offering of a corporation's securities.

Take a Position   (1) To hold securities, in either a long or short position. (2) To purchase securities as a long-term investment.

Takedown   (1) In a municipal underwriting, the price that syndicate members pay when they take bonds from the account. (2) In an underwriting, the number of securities that a syndicate member is supposed to sell.

Take Delivery   In securities, accepting a receipt of stock or bond certificates after they have been purchased or transferred between accounts.

TAN   See *Tax Anticipation Note.*

Tape   A financial news service that reports the prices and sizes of transactions. Although this information was once reported on a paper tape from a "ticker tape" machine, it is now displayed on electronic screens. The name "tape," however, persists.

Tax Anticipation Bills (TAB)   Treasury bills with maturity dates fixed several days after a major tax payment date with a proviso enabling their holders to tender them at face value in satisfaction of their tax requirement and earn a little extra interest in the process.

Tax Anticipation Note (TAN)   A short-term municipal note usually offered on a discount basis. The proceeds of a forthcoming tax collection are pledged to repay the note.

Tax-Exempted Securities   Obligations issued by a state or municipality, or a state or local agency, whose interest payments (but not profits from purchase or sale) are exempted from federal taxation. The interest payment may be exempted from local taxation, too, if purchased by a resident of the issuing state. The term does not include U.S. government obligations. See *General Obligation (GO) Bond; Revenue Bond.*

Tennessee Valley Authority (TVA)   A government-sponsored agency whose bonds are redeemable from the proceeds of the various power projects in the Tennessee River area. Interest payments on these bonds are fully taxable to investors.

Ten Percent Guideline   Formula used in municipal debt issues analysis. The total bonded debt of a municipality shouldn't exceed 10% of the market value of the real estate within the municipality.

Term Bond   (1) A U.S. Treasury bond with a call privilege that becomes effective generally five years prior to maturity. (2) A large municipal bond issue with all the bonds maturing on the same date.

Term Repo   A repurchase agreement whose life extends beyond the normal overnight agreement.

Thin Market   See *Narrow Market*.

Thirty-Day Visible Supply   Calendar published each Thursday by the *Daily Bond Buyer* listing new negotiated and competitive municipal securities that will come to market within the next 30 days.

Three-Handed Deal   Colloquial expression for a municipal security issue underwriting consisting of serial maturities with two term maturities.

Thrift Institutions   Savings bonds, savings and loans, or credit unions. Also known as thrifts.

Throwaway Offer   A nominal (approximate) bid or offer that should not be considered final.

Tight Market   An active, vigorous market with narrow bid-offer spreads.

Tight Money   An economic condition characterized by scarce credit, generally the result of a money supply restricted by the Federal Reserve. See *Easy Money*.

Time Deposit   An account containing a currency balance pledged to remain at that bank for a specified, extended period in return for payment of interest.

Tombstone   The type of newspaper advertisement used for public offering. The ad simply and durably lists all the facts about the issue. Also called the offering circular.

Trade Date   The date a trade was entered into, as opposed to settlement date.

Trader   A person or firm engaged in the business of buying and selling securities, options, or commodities for a profit.

Treasury Bill   A federal bearer obligation issued in denominations of $10,000 to $1 million with a maturity date usually of three months to one year. It is fully marketable at a discount from face value (which determines the interest rate). See *Tax Anticipation Bill*.

Treasury Bond   A federal registered or bearer obligation issued in denominations of $500 to $1 million with maturities ranging from 5 to 35 years, carrying a fixed interest rate and issued, quoted, and traded as a percentage of its face value. See *Flower Bond; Term Bond.*

Treasury Note   A federal registered or bearer obligation issued in denominations of $1,000 to $500 million for maturities of 1 to 10 years, carrying a fixed rate of interest. These notes are issued, quoted, and traded at a percentage of their face value.

Treasury Securities   Debt obligations that the U.S. government issues and that the Treasury Department sells in the form of bills, notes, and bonds.

Turkey   A security that is not doing an investor any good.

TVA   See *Tennessee Valley Authority.*

Twenty-Day (Cooling-off) Period   A period of 20 calendar days following the filing of a registration statement with the SEC, during which (1) the SEC examines the statement for deficiencies, (2) the issuing corporation negotiates with an underwriting syndicate for a final agreement, and (3) the syndicate prepares for the successful distribution of the impending issue. The final day of the period is normally considered the effective date.

Twenty-five Percent Rule   In municipal securities analysis, a rule-of-thumb that an issuer's bonded debt should not exceed 25% of its annual budget.

Twenty-Five Percent Cushion Rule   In the analysis of municipal revenue bonds, a rule-of-thumb that the revenue from the facility built with the bond issue's proceeds should exceed the cost of operations, maintenance, and debt service by 25%.

Undervalued   A term used to describe a security that is trading at a lower price than it should. See *Overvalued.*

Underwriter   Also known as an "investment banker" or "distributor," a middleman between an issuing corporation and the public. The underwriter usually forms an underwriting group, called a syndicate, to limit risk and commitment of capital. He or she may also contract with selling groups to help distribute the issue—for a concession. In the distribution of mutual funds, the underwriter may also be known as a "sponsor," "distributor," or even "wholesaler." Investment bankers also offer other services, such as advice and counsel on the raising and investment of capital.

Underwriter's Retention   The percentage of total issue to which each member of an underwriter's group is entitled and which he or she distributes to customers. The retained amount is usually equal to about 75% of the member's total financial commitment. The syndicate manager decides, on behalf of the other members, how to distribute the rest of the issue, (or "the pot") and how it is to be sold to institutional investors (group sales) or reversed for handling by selling groups. See *Philadelphia Plan; Western Account.*

Underwriting Agreement The contract between the investment banker and the corporation, containing the final terms and prices of the issue. It is signed either on the evening before or early in the morning of the public offering date (effective date).

Underwriting Compensation (Spread) The gross profit realized by an underwriter equal to the difference between the price paid to the issuing corporation and the price of the public offering.

Undivided Account In an underwriting agreement, an arrangement for the sharing of liability in which each member of the syndicate is liable for any unsold portion of an issue. The degree of liability is based on each member's percentage participation. See *Syndicate.*

Uniform Practice Code ("The Code") A code established and maintained by the NASD Board of Governors that regulates the mechanics of executing and completing securities transactions in the OTC market.

Uniform Practice Committee An NASD district subcommittee that disseminates information and interpretations handed down by the Board of Governors regarding the Uniform Practice Code.

Unlisted Security A security that is not traded on an exchange. Usually called an over-the-counter security.

Unqualified Legal (Clean) Opinion An unconditional affirmation of a security's legality, rendered either before or after the security is sold. See *Qualified Legal Opinion.*

Unsecured Obligation (Bond) A debt instrument whose repayment is backed solely by the creditworthiness of the issuer. No specific property is pledged as security. Also called a "debenture."

Upgrade Raising a security's rating by improving the credit quality of the issuer or issue.

Uptrend Any generally upward movement in a security's price.

U.S. Government Securities Debt issues of the U.S. government (Treasury Department), backed by the government's unlimited power of taxation, such as Treasury bills, notes, bonds, and Series EE and Series HH bonds.

Variable Rate Interest rate on a security that is subject to change, commonly in connection with the rates paid on selected issues of Treasury securities. Also called floating rate.

Vault Cash All the cash in a bank's vault.

Velocity (of Money) The number of times a dollar changes hands in one year. Given a fixed money supply, increased velocity is usually a sign to the Federal Reserve that an increase in the money supply is needed.

Visible Supply See *Thirty-Day Visible Supply.*

Volume Number of bonds or shares traded during specific periods, such as daily, weekly, or monthly.

Voluntary Underwriter An individual or corporation that purchases a security from an issuer or affiliated person and offers it for public sale under an effective registration statement.

Weak Market A market characterized by a greater number of sellers than buyers, which creates a general downtrend in prices.

Western Account An agreement among underwriters regarding liability, in which each member of the syndicate is liable only for the amount of its participation in, but not for the unsold portion of, the issue. See *Syndicate.*

When Issued/When Distributred Contract A delivery contract involving securities (stocks or bonds) that have been proposed for distribution but not yet issued. The date of delivery is set for some time in the future by the NASD Uniform Practice Committee or the appropriate stock exchange, as the case may be.

Wholesaler See *Underwriter.*

Whoops Securities of the Washington Public Power Supply System (WPPS).

WI See *When Issued.*

Window Settlement Transactions that are not cleared through the SCC or NCC and that are completed in the office of the purchasing firm by means of certificate delivery versus immediate payment.

Workout Market In the OTC market, a range of prices quoted by a market maker who is not certain that a market is available, but who feels he or she can "work one out" within a reasonable period of time.

Yankee CD A dollar-dominated, foreign-issued time deposit that is registered for sale in the United States.

Yankee Bond A dollar-denominated, foreign-issued bond that is registered for sale in the United States.

Yellow Sheets A daily publication of the National Quotation Bureau giving markets in corporate debt securities. See *Pink Sheets.*

Yield (Rate of Return) The percentage return on an investor's money in terms of current prices. It is the annual dividend/interest per share of bond, divided by the current market price of that security.

Yield Curve Graph depicting the relation of interest rates to time: time is plotted on the X-axis and yields on the Y-axis. The curve shows whether short-term interest rates are higher or lower than long-term rates. A positive yield curve results if short-term rates are lower, and a negative yield curve results if short-term rates are higher. A flat yield curve results if long- and short-term rates do not differ greatly. Generally, the yield curve is positive because investors tie up their money for longer periods and are rewarded with better yields.

Yield to Maturity The calculation of an average rate of return on a bond (with a maturity over one year) if it is held to its maturity date and if all cash flows are reinvested at the same rate of interest. It includes an adjustment for any premium paid or discount received. It is a calculation used to compare relative values of bonds.

Zero-Coupon Discount Security A debt security that offers no payments of interest, only payment of full face value at maturity that is used at a deep discount from face value.

Index